RSPT

Assessin
verbal a
nonverb
abilitie
Ages
7–12

CW01583311

MANUAL for STAGE TWO of the Reasoning Progress Tests

Denis Vincent & Mary Crumpler

RSPT

Assessing verbal and nonverbal abilities
Ages 7–12

MANUAL

for STAGE TWO of the Reasoning Progress Tests

Denis Vincent & Mary Crumpler
East London Assessment Group, University of East London

Hodder & Stoughton
A MEMBER OF THE HODDER HEADLINE GROUP

About this manual

This manual gives instructions for administering, marking and interpreting the results of Stage Two of the *Reasoning Progress Tests*:

- Verbal Test 3 – for ages 6:11 to 9:4
- Nonverbal Test 3 – for ages 6:11 to 9:4
- Verbal Test 4 – for ages 7:11 to 10:4
- Nonverbal Test 4 – for ages 7:11 to 10:4
- Verbal Test 5 – for ages 8:11 to 11:4
- Nonverbal Test 5 – for ages 8:11 to 11:4
- Verbal Test 6 – for ages 9:11 to 12:4
- Nonverbal Test 6 – for ages 9:11 to 12:4.

A separate manual is provided for use with Stage One of the *Reasoning Progress Tests*, assessing verbal and nonverbal reasoning in Years 1 and 2.

The *Reasoning Progress Tests* are suitable for use alongside the *Reading Progress Tests* and the *Numeracy Progress Tests*, by the same authors, as part of a year-on-year progress monitoring programme.

For details of the *Reading Progress Tests* and the *Numeracy Progress Tests*, and to view demos of the accompanying *Scorer/Profiler CD-ROMs*, visit www.hoddertests.co.uk.

ISBN 0 340 85893 1
First published 2002

Impression number 10 9 8 7 6 5 4 3 2 1
Year 2007 2006 2005 2004 2003 2002

Printed in Great Britain for Hodder & Stoughton Educational, the educational publishing division of Hodder Headline Plc, 338 Euston Road, London NW1 3BH, by Hobbs the Printers, Totton, Hampshire SO40 3WX.

Contents

Introduction

The Reasoning Progress Tests (RsPT)

The *Reasoning Progress Tests* are a series of reasoning tests for ages 5–11. The tests were developed by the East London Assessment Group at the University of East London, on behalf of Hodder & Stoughton Educational.

The series is published in two Stages:

- **Stage One** of the series is designed for use with pupils aged 5–8 (Key Stage One of the national curriculum for England and Wales) and comprises a Picture Test, Verbal Test 2 and Nonverbal Test 2;

- **Stage Two** of the series is designed for use with pupils aged 7–12 (Key Stage Two of the national curriculum for England and Wales) and comprises Verbal Tests 3 to 6 and Nonverbal Tests 3 to 6, for Years 3 to 6.

The two Stages have separate manuals containing administration and marking instructions for all of the tests in that Stage, together with conversion tables giving standardised scores and percentiles, expected national curriculum levels for given levels of reasoning ability and guidance for interpretation.

The *Reasoning Progress Tests* thus provide continuous year-on-year measures of verbal and nonverbal reasoning across the primary years, and allow teachers to choose whether to use either or both measures (see page 5). They are thorough while being quick and relatively undemanding to administer. The tests are objectively marked and employ a comprehensive selection of the standard question formats used in testing verbal and non-verbal reasoning.

The tests are untimed, but can normally be administered in 30–40 minutes. The pace is set by the teacher, who will need to ensure that all the pupils are given sufficient time to answer each question. For convenience of administration, the tests are designed to be used with whole classes of pupils or with large groups, although they can be used with individuals or small groups if this is more appropriate for certain pupils.

Cross-sectional norms based on the reasoning ability of representative samples of pupils in schools throughout England, Wales, Scotland and Northern Ireland tested in 2001 and 2002 are provided for each test (more details are given on page 40). In Stage Two, standardised scores are provided for successive Reasoning Tests (verbal and nonverbal) in, respectively, age ranges 6:11–9:4 (Test 3); 7:11–10:4 (Test 4); 8:11–11:4 (Test 5); 9:11–12:4 (Test 6). The tests are designed for use at any time during the school year, as appropriate to the purpose in testing.

The *Reasoning Progress Tests* are intended for all of the principal uses in educational screening, monitoring and guidance for which reasoning tests are normally employed. Important examples include:

- identification of pupils whose ability and educational potential have not been previously recognised;

- detection of pupils who may be under-achieving, where there is a substantial mismatch between their ability and their school attainment;
- evaluation of performance of individuals or groups of pupils in the light of their underlying ability and potential.

Please note, however, that these tests have *not* been designed for academic selection purposes.

Selecting a test: verbal or nonverbal?

Verbal and nonverbal tests provide different ways of measuring general underlying cognitive ability. Both types of test were found to correlate well with attainment tests in the course of the validation research carried out during the development of the *Reasoning Progress Tests* (pages 55–6). However, as is commonly found in such research, the verbal tests were somewhat more highly correlated with educational attainment. Where scope for testing is limited, the appropriate verbal test will thus usually be the test of choice.

Nevertheless, there will be many situations in which a nonverbal test is to be preferred – for example, where a reading-free format is desirable or where it is necessary to avoid, or at least minimise, reliance on knowledge of spoken English. Moreover, it is possible that non-verbal tests may be indicative of potential in areas other than those where language is central or which involve logical problem-solving skills and lie outside conventional academic subjects.

Using both a verbal and nonverbal test will provide a fuller sampling of a pupil's cognitive ability, and is thus recommended best practice. Nonverbal assessment may, however, add a unique element to the validity of the assessment. Although in most cases a moderate to high degree of agreement is to be expected, unusual contrasts can be instructive. Children with (perhaps undetected) specific reading difficulties, for example, may be found to perform relatively well on nonverbal, as opposed to verbal, tests.

Group size
The test is designed to be administered to whole classes or large groups. If you wish, you may vary this, depending on the independence of the pupils concerned, testing in small groups or individually, as appropriate.

Timing
No time limit is set for the test, but most pupils will complete it within 30–40 minutes. However, the pupils should not be given a strict time limit, but allowed as much time as they need to attempt all the questions.

Preparation
Each pupil will need:

- a copy of the test booklet;
- a pencil.

You will need a copy of the test as well as these instructions.

Test conditions
It is important that the pupils complete their answers without discussion, collaboration or copying. However, if a pupil needs additional explanation in order to understand how to answer the questions, you may give this.

Method of answering
All the questions are answered by drawing a line under the chosen answer. If the pupils you are working with are used to indicating their answers by some other means (for example, by drawing a ring round their chosen answer) rather than by underlining, they may answer in this way. The instructions you give the pupils will need to be modified accordingly.

Answers may be altered by rubbing or crossing out.

Question numbers
The pupils' test booklets contain question numbers. These are included to make marking easier. You should not refer pupils to them when working through the test.

Giving the test
Suggested wording for you to use when explaining the questions is given in *italics*. You do not need to keep to this verbatim – the most important thing is that the pupils know what they have to do. As you introduce each new section, pause to give them time to read through the printed instructions before you start working through the practice example.

Be as encouraging as possible, but do not give feedback as to whether answers are right or wrong.

Give each pupil a copy of the test booklet.

Ask the pupils to write their name in the appropriate place. (If you wish, the pupils can continue to fill in the required details, or an adult can complete these.) Explain how the pupils are to answer the questions – by drawing a line under the answer they have chosen. If they wish to change an answer, they should cross or rub out their original answer and draw a line under their new choice.

In this booklet, there are five different sorts of questions for you to answer.

Turn over and look at the first question. Here you have to make two new words. You make the first by taking ***one*** *letter away from the first word in* ***bold****. You make the second by adding that letter to the second word in* ***bold****. Then you have to draw lines under the two new words you have made, one from each set of brackets.*

We're going to do the first question together.

Look at the two words in bold type, ***scream*** *and* ***table****. Then look at the words in brackets – (****scram crams cream crease****) in the first set of brackets and (****stable sable tablet cable****) in the second set of brackets. Find the only word in each set of brackets that can be made by taking a letter from* ***scream*** *and adding it to* ***table****.*

The answer is ***cream*** *and* ***stable****. You can take away the letter* ***s*** *from* ***scream*** *and add it to* ***table*** *to make* ***cream*** *and* ***stable****. So draw a line under* ***cream*** *and a line under* ***stable****.*

Check that the pupils have understood what they have to do.

Answer the questions on the next page in the same way, and then wait until I tell you to turn over.

Check that the pupils have completed the page.

Turn over and look at the sentences on the next page. In every sentence, there is one place where there are four words in brackets. You have to read the words and then draw a line under the word that fits into the sentence.

Let's read the first sentence together.
*Clock is to hours as calendar is to (****pictures months birthdays organise****).*

The word that fits the sentence is ***months*** *because a clock shows time passing in hours and a calendar in months. So draw a line under* ***months****.*

Check that the pupils have understood what they have to do.

Answer the rest of the questions on this page in the same way.

Check that the pupils have completed the page.

Now look at the next page. In each question, there are two words with a question mark between them, followed by four other words. You have to find the word that should replace the question mark and then draw a line under that word. The 'rule' is that a single letter changes in the first word to get to the middle word and then another letter changes in the middle word to get to the third word.

Let's do one together.

Look at the first question.
break - ? - cream ***brake bread creak wreak.***

The answer is ***creak****, because the 'b' in break changes to a 'c' to make creak and then the 'k' in creak changes to an 'm' to make cream, and all the other letters remain the same. Draw a line under* ***creak****.*

Check that the pupils have understood what they have to do.

Answer the rest of the questions on this page in the same way, and then wait until I tell you to turn over.

Check that the pupils have completed the page.

Turn over and look at the next page. In each question there is a word followed by four pictures. You have to find the picture that matches the word and then draw a line under the picture you have chosen.

We're going to do one together.

*Look at the first word '****domestic****'. Which picture illustrates domestic? The dog is the domestic animal, so draw a line under the dog.*

Check that the pupils have understood what they have to do.

Answer the rest of the questions on this page in the same way.

Check that the pupils have completed the page.

Let's look at the next page. In every line of words, there is a general word and five examples of it. You have to find the general word and then draw a line under it.

We're going to do the first one together.

Let's read it – ***sense smell touch sight hearing taste***

*The general word is '****sense****' and* ***smell, touch, sight, hearing*** *and* ***taste*** *are all examples of our senses. Draw a line under '****sense****'.*

Check that the pupils have understood what they have to do.

Now answer the rest of the questions on this page in the same way.

Check that the pupils have completed the test and then collect in the test booklets ready for marking.

Administration

Group size
The test is designed to be administered to whole classes or large groups. If you wish, you may vary this, depending on the independence of the pupils concerned, testing in small groups or individually, as appropriate.

Timing
No time limit is set for the test, but most pupils will complete it within 30–40 minutes. However, the pupils should not be given a strict time limit, but allowed as much time as they need to attempt all the questions.

Preparation
Each pupil will need:

- a copy of the test booklet;
- a pencil.

You will need a copy of the test as well as these instructions.

Test conditions
It is important that the pupils complete their answers without discussion, collaboration or copying. However, if a pupil needs additional explanation in order to understand how to answer the questions, you may give this.

Method of answering
All the questions are answered by drawing a line under the chosen answer. If the pupils you are working with are used to indicating their answers by some other means (for example, by drawing a ring round their chosen answer) rather than by underlining, they may answer in this way. The instructions you give the pupils will need to be modified accordingly.

Answers may be altered by rubbing or crossing out.

Question numbers
The pupils' test booklets contain question numbers. These are included to make marking easier. You should not refer pupils to them when working through the test.

Giving the test
Suggested wording for you to use when explaining the questions is given in *italics*. You do not need to keep to this verbatim – the most important thing is that the pupils know what they have to do. As you introduce each new section, pause to give them time to read through the printed instructions before you start working through the practice example.

Be as encouraging as possible, but do not give feedback as to whether answers are right or wrong.

Give each pupil a copy of the test booklet.

Ask the pupils to write their name in the appropriate place. (If you wish, the pupils can continue to fill in the required details, or an adult can complete these.) Explain how the pupils are to answer the questions – by drawing a line under the answer they have chosen. If they wish to change an answer, they should cross or rub out their original answer and draw a line under their new choice.

In this booklet, there are four different sorts of questions for you to answer.

Look at the first question. There are two sets of shapes. You have to look at the three shapes in the box on the left and then find the shape from the box on the right which is most like the first three shapes.

We're going to do the first one together.

Look at the three shapes in the box on the left. Now look at the five shapes in the box on the right. Which of the five shapes in the box on the right is most like the first three shapes?

*It's the fifth shape, shape **E**, because it has three straight sides and one curved side, just like the first three shapes. So draw a line under shape **E**.*

Check that the pupils have understood what they have to do.

Turn over and answer the questions on the next two pages in the same way and then wait until I tell you to turn over.

Check that all the pupils have completed the two pages.

Turn over and look at the next page. Here you have to imagine that the shape in the box on the left has been folded along the dotted line. Then you have to decide which of the five shapes in the box on the right it would look like after it has been folded.

We're going to do the first one together.

*Look at the first shape and look at the position of the dotted line. If the shape were folded along the dotted line, which of the shapes in the box on the right would it look like? It would be like the second shape, shape **B**, so draw a line under that shape.*

Check that the pupils have understood what they have to do.

Now answer the rest of the questions on this page and the questions on the next page in the same way and then wait until I tell you to turn over.

Check that the pupils have completed the two pages.

Turn over and look at the next page. Here you have to find the picture in each question that is the 'odd one out' and draw a line under it.

Look at the first sets of shapes. Which set is the 'odd one out', the set that is most different from the others?

*All the sets have three white shapes on the bottom row and one purple shape above the first white shape except the third set, set **C**, which has a purple and a white shape on each row, making that the odd one out. So draw a line under set **C**.*

Check that the pupils have understood what they have to do.

Answer the rest of the questions on this page in the same way.

Check that all the pupils have completed the page.

Look at the questions on the next page. There are some patterns for you to look at. Each pattern in the boxes on the left has a question mark to show where a piece of the pattern is missing. You have to look at the shapes on the right to find the missing piece and draw a line under it.

We're going to do the first one together.

*Look at the pattern in the first box on the left. There is a piece missing from the pattern. Look at the patterns on the right. Which one is the missing piece? The answer is the first piece, piece **A**, because that completes the pattern of the squares. So draw a line under piece **A**.*

Check that the pupils have understood what they have to do.

Now answer the rest of the questions in the booklet in the same way.

Check that the pupils have completed the test and then collect in the booklets for marking.

Group size
The test is designed to be administered to whole classes or large groups. If you wish, you may vary this, depending on the independence of the pupils concerned, testing in small groups or individually, as appropriate.

Timing
No time limit is set for the test, but most pupils will complete it within 30–40 minutes. However, the pupils should not be given a strict time limit, but allowed as much time as they need to attempt all the questions.

Preparation
Each pupil will need:

- a copy of the test booklet;
- a pencil.

You will need a copy of the test as well as these instructions.

Test conditions
It is important that the pupils complete their answers without discussion, collaboration or copying. However, if a pupil needs additional explanation in order to understand how to answer the questions, you may give this.

Method of answering
All the questions are answered by drawing a line under the chosen answer. If the pupils you are working with are used to indicating their answers by some other means (for example, by drawing a ring round their chosen answer) rather than by underlining, they may answer in this way. The instructions you give the pupils will need to be modified accordingly.

Answers may be altered by rubbing or crossing out.

Question numbers
The pupils' test booklets contain question numbers. These are included to make marking easier. You should not refer pupils to them when working through the test.

Giving the test
Suggested wording for you to use when explaining the questions is given in *italics*. You do not need to keep to this verbatim – the most important thing is that the pupils know what they have to do. As you introduce each new section, pause to give them time to read through the printed instructions before you start working through the practice example.

Be as encouraging as possible, but do not give feedback as to whether answers are right or wrong.

Give each pupil a copy of the test booklet.

Ask the pupils to write their name in the appropriate place. (If you wish, the pupils can continue to fill in the required details, or an adult can complete these.) Explain how the pupils are to answer the questions – by drawing a line under the answer they have chosen. If they wish to change an answer, they should cross or rub out their original answer and draw a line under their new choice.

In this booklet, there are four different sorts of questions for you to answer.

Turn over and look at the first question. There is a set of words and one of them does not fit with the others – it is the odd one out. You have to find the odd one out and then draw a line under that word.

We're going to do the first one together.

The four words are ***square rectangle cube hexagon****. The odd one out is* ***cube*** *because* ***square****,* ***rectangle*** *and* ***hexagon*** *are all two-dimensional shapes, but a* ***cube*** *is three-dimensional. So draw a line under* ***cube****.*

Check that the pupils have understood what they have to do.

Now answer the questions on this page and the next page in the same way, and then wait until I tell you to turn over.

Check that the pupils have completed the two pages.

Turn over and look at the next page. In each question there is a word followed by four pictures. You have to find the picture that matches the word, and then draw a line under the picture you have chosen.

We're going to do the first one together.

Look at the first word ***helmet****. Which picture shows a helmet? It's the fourth picture, picture* ***D****, so draw a line under that picture.*

Check that the pupils have understood what they have to do.

Answer the rest of the questions on this page in the same way.

Check that the pupils have completed the page.

Now look at the questions on the next page. Here you have to make two new words. You make the first by taking ***one*** *letter away from the first word in* ***bold****. You make the second by adding that letter to the second word in* ***bold****. Then you have to draw lines under the two new words you have made, one from each set of brackets.*

We're going to do the first one together.

*Look at the first two words in bold type, **shake** and **tick**. Then look at the words in brackets – (**snake hake awake ask**) in the first set of brackets and (**lick tickle stock stick**) in the second set of brackets. Find the only word in each set of brackets that can be made by taking a letter from **shake** and adding it to **tick**.*

*The answer is **hake** and **stick**. You can take away the letter **s** from **shake** and add it to **tick** to make **hake** and **stick**. So draw a line under **hake** and a line under **stick**.*

Check that the pupils have understood what they have to do.

Answer the questions on this page and the next page in the same way.

Check that the pupils have completed the two pages.

Now look at the sentences on the next page. In every sentence, there is at least one place where there are four words in brackets. You have to read the words and then draw a line under the word that fits into the sentence.

Let's read the first sentence together.
*Brick is to wall as tile is to (**chimney window roof porch**).*

*The word that fits the sentence is **roof** because a wall is made of bricks and a roof is made of tiles. So draw a line under **roof**.*

Check that the pupils have understood what they have to do.

Answer the rest of the questions on this page in the same way.

Check that the pupils have completed the test and then collect in the booklets for marking.

Group size
The test is designed to be administered to whole classes or large groups. If you wish, you may vary this, depending on the independence of the pupils concerned, testing in small groups or individually, as appropriate.

Timing
No time limit is set for the test, but most pupils will complete it within 30–40 minutes. However, the pupils should not be given a strict time limit, but allowed as much time as they need to attempt all the questions.

Preparation
Each pupil will need:

- a copy of the test booklet;
- a pencil.

You will need a copy of the test as well as these instructions.

Test conditions
It is important that the pupils complete their answers without discussion, collaboration or copying. However, if a pupil needs additional explanation in order to understand how to answer the questions, you may give this.

Method of answering
All the questions are answered by drawing a line under the chosen answer. If the pupils you are working with are used to indicating their answers by some other means (for example, by drawing a ring round their chosen answer) rather than by underlining, they may answer in this way. The instructions you give the pupils will need to be modified accordingly.

Answers may be altered by rubbing or crossing out.

Question numbers
The pupils' test booklets contain question numbers. These are included to make marking easier. You should not refer pupils to them when working through the test.

Giving the test
Suggested wording for you to use when explaining the questions is given in *italics*. You do not need to keep to this verbatim – the most important thing is that the pupils know what they have to do. As you introduce each new section, pause to give them time to read through the printed instructions before you start working through the practice example.

Be as encouraging as possible, but do not give feedback as to whether answers are right or wrong.

Give each pupil a copy of the test booklet.

Ask the pupils to write their name in the appropriate place. (If you wish, the pupils can continue to fill in the required details, or an adult can complete these.) Explain how the pupils are to answer the questions – by drawing a line under the answer they have chosen. If they wish to change an answer, they should cross or rub out their original answer and draw a line under their new choice.

In this booklet, there are four different sorts of questions for you to answer.

Turn over and look at the first question. Here there are two sets of shapes. You have to look at the three shapes in the box on the left and then find the shape from the box on the right which is most like the first three shapes.

We're going to do the first one together.

Look at the three arrows in the box on the left. Now look at the five arrows in the box on the right. Which of the five arrows in the box on the right is most like the first three arrows?

*It's the fourth arrow, arrow **D**, because it is facing towards the left in the same way as the first three arrows. So draw a line under arrow **D**.*

Check that the pupils have understood what they have to do.

Answer the questions on this page and the next page in the same way, and then wait until I tell you to turn over.

Check that all the pupils have completed the two pages.

Turn over and look at the next page. Here you have to find the shape or pattern in each question that fits into the space with the question mark.

We're going to do the first one together.

Look at the top row of boxes. Four of the boxes have sets of shapes in them and one has a question mark. The sets of shapes in the boxes are in an order. Look at the sets of shapes on the right and decide which set should go in the box with the question mark. Then draw a line under that set.

*One extra shape has been added each time – in the first box there is a triangle with a circle in front of it and in the second box a square has been added. In the fourth box there are two extra circles and in the fifth box yet another circle has been added. The answer is **D**, where there is the same triangle, circle and square as in the second box, plus one of the circles that have appeared by the fourth box. So draw a line under **D**.*

Check that the pupils have understood what they have to do.

Answer the questions on this page and the next page in the same way, and then wait until I tell you to turn over.

Check that all the pupils have completed the two pages.

Turn over and look at the questions on the next page. There are sequences of four numbers, followed by a question mark. There are then a further four numbers and you have to work out which of these comes next in the sequence.

Look at the first one – ***10, 8, 6, 4****. Which number comes next?* ***2, 3, 1*** *or* ***5****?*

The sequence ***10, 8, 6, 4*** *follows a rule. You have to discover the rule and then work out which number comes next.*

In this case the numbers go down by 2 each time. 10 take away 2 equals 8, 8 take away 2 equals 6, 6 take away 2 equals 4, and 4 take away 2 equals 2, so you should draw a line under the number 2.

For each question, you need to work out the rule – it will not always be 'take away 2'.

Check that the pupils have understood what they have to do.

Answer the rest of the questions on this page in the same way.

Check that all the pupils have completed the page.

Look at the questions on the next page. There are some patterns for you to look at. Each pattern in the boxes on the left has a question mark to show where a piece of the pattern is missing. You have to look at the shapes on the right to find the missing piece and draw a line under it.

We're going to do the first one together.

Look at the pattern in the first box on the left. There is a piece missing from the pattern. Look at the patterns on the right. Which one is the missing piece? The answer is the first piece, piece ***A****, because that completes the pattern of the lines. So draw a line under piece* ***A****.*

Check that the pupils have understood what they have to do.

Now answer the rest of the questions in the booklet in the same way. Make sure that you turn over and answer the questions on the back cover.

Check that the pupils have completed the test and then collect in the booklets for marking.

Group size
The test is designed to be administered to whole classes or large groups. If you wish, you may vary this, depending on the independence of the pupils concerned, testing in small groups or individually, as appropriate.

Timing
No time limit is set for the test, but most pupils will complete it within 30–40 minutes. However, the pupils should not be given a strict time limit, but allowed as much time as they need to attempt all the questions.

Preparation
Each pupil will need:

- a copy of the test booklet;
- a pencil.

You will need a copy of the test as well as these instructions.

Test conditions
It is important that the pupils complete their answers without discussion, collaboration or copying. However, if a pupil needs additional explanation in order to understand how to answer the questions, you may give this.

Method of answering
All the questions are answered by drawing a line under the chosen answer. If the pupils you are working with are used to indicating their answers by some other means (for example, by drawing a ring round their chosen answer) rather than by underlining, they may answer in this way. The instructions you give the pupils will need to be modified accordingly.

Answers may be altered by rubbing or crossing out.

Question numbers
The pupils' test booklets contain question numbers. These are included to make marking easier. You should not refer pupils to them when working through the test.

Giving the test
Suggested wording for you to use when explaining the questions is given in *italics*. You do not need to keep to this verbatim – the most important thing is that the pupils know what they have to do. As you introduce each new section, pause to give them time to read through the printed instructions before you start working through the practice example.

Be as encouraging as possible, but do not give feedback as to whether answers are right or wrong.

Give each pupil a copy of the test booklet.

Ask the pupils to write their name in the appropriate place. (If you wish, the pupils can continue to fill in the required details, or an adult can complete these.) Explain how the pupils are to answer the questions – by drawing a line under the answer they have chosen. If they wish to change an answer, they should cross or rub out their original answer and draw a line under their new choice.

In this booklet, there are five different sorts of questions for you to answer.

Turn over and look at the first question. There is a word followed by four pictures. You have to find the picture that matches the word, and then draw a line under the picture you have chosen.

We're going to do the first one together.

Look at the first word ***transparent****. Which picture illustrates transparent? It's the window, picture* ***B****, so draw a line under the window.*

Check that the pupils have understood what they have to do.

Answer the rest of the questions on this page in the same way.

Check that the pupils have completed the page.

Look at the questions on the next page. In each question, there is a word printed in ***bold****, followed by four words in brackets. You have to find the word in brackets that is most similar in meaning to the word in* ***bold****, and then draw a line under that word.*

Let's look at the first one together.

The word in bold is ***anxiety*** *and the words in brackets are* ***pulse nerves worry calm****. The most similar word to* ***anxiety*** *is* ***worry****. So draw a line under* ***worry****.*

Check that the pupils have understood what they have to do.

Answer the rest of the questions on this page in the same way and then wait until I tell you to turn over.

Check that the pupils have completed the page.

Turn over and look at the questions at the top of the next page. In every question, there is a sentence with part of one word missing. Then there are four words, one of which will complete the part-word in the sentence so that it makes sense. You have to find the correct word and then draw a line under it.

Look at the first one.
*It's very busy in the s****hip****ping centre /s****hop****ping centre /s****lip****ping centre /s****top****ping centre at*

weekends.

*The answer is s**hop**ping – It's very busy in the s**hop**ping centre at weekends. – so draw a line under **hop** as this is the word that completes the part-word in the sentence.*

Check that the pupils have understood what they have to do.

Answer the other three questions in this section in the same way.

Check that the pupils have completed the section.

Look down to the next section. In each sentence, there is at least one place where there are four words in brackets. You have to read the words and then draw a line under the word that fits into the sentence.

Let's read the first sentence together.
*Bridge is to cross as mountain is to (**hill climb lake countryside**).*

*The word that fits the sentence is **climb**. Just as you cross a bridge, you climb a mountain – both **cross** and **climb** are verbs. So draw a line under **climb**.*

Check that the pupils have understood what they have to do.

Answer the questions on the next page in the same way, and then wait until I tell you to turn over.

Check that the pupils have completed the page.

*Turn over and look at the questions on the next page. There are some sentences printed in **bold** which have four other sentences underneath them. You have to read the sentences and then draw a line under the only sentence that you can be **sure** is true.*

Look at the first sentences in bold.
Salim is going to work to become a chef. To become a chef you have to train for three years.

Now let's read the four sentences underneath.
Salim has decided it takes too long to become a chef.
Salim is going to train for three years.
Salim is already a good cook.
Salim's Dad cooks for him at home.

*The first sentence in bold tells us that Salim wants to become a chef and the second sentence tells us that a chef's training takes three years. Therefore Salim is going to train for three years, making sentence **B** the right answer. So draw a line under sentence **B**.*

Check that the pupils have understood what they have to do.

Now answer the questions on this page and the next page in the same way.

Check that the pupils have completed the test and then collect in the booklets for marking.

(When totalling each pupil's marks, take care to include Questions 11–13 where the recording box is part-way down the page.)

Group size
The test is designed to be administered to whole classes or large groups. If you wish, you may vary this, depending on the independence of the pupils concerned, testing in small groups or individually, as appropriate.

Timing
No time limit is set for the test, but most pupils will complete it within 30–40 minutes. However, the pupils should not be given a strict time limit, but allowed as much time as they need to attempt all the questions.

Preparation
Each pupil will need:

- a copy of the test booklet;
- a pencil.

You will need a copy of the test as well as these instructions.

Test conditions
It is important that the pupils complete their answers without discussion, collaboration or copying. However, if a pupil needs additional explanation in order to understand how to answer the questions, you may give this.

Method of answering
All the questions are answered by drawing a line under the chosen answer. If the pupils you are working with are used to indicating their answers by some other means (for example, by drawing a ring round their chosen answer) rather than by underlining, they may answer in this way. The instructions you give the pupils will need to be modified accordingly.

Answers may be altered by rubbing or crossing out.

Question numbers
The pupils' test booklets contain question numbers. These are included to make marking easier. You should not refer pupils to them when working through the test.

Giving the test
Suggested wording for you to use when explaining the questions is given in *italics*. You do not need to keep to this verbatim – the most important thing is that the pupils know what they have to do. As you introduce each new section, pause to give them time to read through the printed instructions before you start working through the practice example.

Be as encouraging as possible, but do not give feedback as to whether answers are right or wrong.

Give each pupil a copy of the test booklet.

Ask the pupils to write their name in the appropriate place. (If you wish, the pupils can continue to fill in the required details, or an adult can complete these.) Explain how the pupils are to answer the questions – by drawing a line under the answer they have chosen. If they wish to change an answer, they should cross or rub out their original answer and draw a line under their new choice.

In this booklet, there are four different sorts of questions for you to answer.

Look at the first question. Here you have to find a 'partner' for the shape or pattern in a box by itself each time.

Look at the two shapes in the first box and decide how they go together. Then look at the third shape, in a box by itself. Which of the five shapes on the right goes with the shape on its own to make a pair, in the same way as the first two shapes? Draw a line under the shape that makes a pair in the same way as the first two shapes.

*The answer is the fifth shape, shape **E**. In the first box, there is an oval with a green circle at the top left followed by an oval at right angles to the first with a wavy line down it and a green circle to the left of the line. The shape in the box by itself is a crescent with a green circle at the top left, so its partner must be the fifth shape, shape **E**, with a crescent at right angles to the first with a wavy line down it and a green circle to the left of the line. So draw a line under shape **E**.*

Check that the pupils have understood what they have to do.

Turn over and answer the questions on the next two pages in the same way, and then wait until I tell you to turn over.

Check that the pupils have completed the questions.

Turn over and look at the next set of questions. Here you have to find the shape in each question that fits into the space with a question mark.

We're going to do the first one together.

Look at the top row of boxes. Four of the boxes have sets of faces in them and one has a question mark. The faces in the boxes are in an order. Look at the sets of faces on the right and decide which set should go in the box with the question mark. Then draw a line under that set.

There is one more face each time. In the first box, there is a row of three faces – happy, expressionless and sad. In the second box, the first row is the same as in the first box and a second row of faces begins, with a happy face. In the third box another face appears in the second row, an expressionless face, just as in the top row. In the fourth box, the second row of faces is completed with a sad face – the two rows of faces are identical. In the fifth box, a set of faces is needed which has two rows of faces the same as in the fourth box, with a *happy face beginning a third row, just like set **B**. So draw a line under set **B**.*

Check that the pupils have understood what they have to do.

Answer the questions on this page and the next page in the same way and then wait until I tell you to turn over.

Check that all the pupils have completed these pages.

Turn over and look at the questions on the next page. There are sequences of four numbers, followed by a question mark. There are then a further four numbers and you have to work out which comes next in the sequence.

*Look at the first one – **1**, **3**, **5**, 7. Which number comes next? **8**, **9**, **6** or **11**?*

*The sequence **1**, **3**, **5**, 7 follows a rule. You have to discover the rule and then work out which number comes next.*

In this case the numbers go up by 2 each time. 1 plus 2 equals 3, 3 plus 2 equals 5, 5 plus 2 equals 7, and 7 plus 2 equals 9, so you should draw a line under the number 9.

For each question, you need to work out the rule – it will not always be 'plus 2'.

Check that the pupils have understood what they have to do.

Answer the rest of the questions on this page in the same way.

Check that all the pupils have completed the page.

Look at the question at the top of the next page. Here you have to imagine that the shape in the box on the left has been folded along the dotted line. Then you have to decide which of the five shapes in the box on the right it would look like after it has been folded.

*Look at the first shape and look at the position of the dotted line. If the shape were folded along the dotted line, which of the shapes in the box on the right would it look like? It would be like the fifth shape, shape **E**, so draw a line under that shape.*

Check that the pupils have understood what they have to do.

Now answer the rest of the questions in the booklet in the same way. Make sure that you turn over and answer the questions on the back cover.

Check that the pupils have completed the test and then collect in the booklets for marking.

Group size
The test is designed to be administered to whole classes or large groups. If you wish, you may vary this, depending on the independence of the pupils concerned, testing in small groups or individually, as appropriate.

Timing
No time limit is set for the test, but most pupils will complete it within 30–40 minutes. However, the pupils should not be given a strict time limit, but allowed as much time as they need to attempt all the questions.

Preparation
Each pupil will need:

- a copy of the test booklet;
- a pencil.

You will need a copy of the test as well as these instructions.

Test conditions
It is important that the pupils complete their answers without discussion, collaboration or copying. However, if a pupil needs additional explanation in order to understand how to answer the questions, you may give this.

Method of answering
All the questions are answered by drawing a line under the chosen answer. If the pupils you are working with are used to indicating their answers by some other means (for example, by drawing a ring round their chosen answer) rather than by underlining, they may answer in this way. The instructions you give the pupils will need to be modified accordingly.

Answers may be altered by rubbing or crossing out.

Question numbers
The pupils' test booklets contain question numbers. These are included to make marking easier. You should not refer pupils to them when working through the test.

Giving the test
Suggested wording for you to use when explaining the questions is given in *italics*. You do not need to keep to this verbatim – the most important thing is that the pupils know what they have to do. As you introduce each new section, pause to give them time to read through the printed instructions before you start working through the practice example.

Be as encouraging as possible, but do not give feedback as to whether answers are right or wrong.

Give each pupil a copy of the test booklet.

Ask the pupils to write their name in the appropriate place. (If you wish, the pupils can continue to fill in the required details, or an adult can complete these.) Explain how the pupils are to answer the questions – by drawing a line under the answer they have chosen. If they wish to change an answer, they should cross or rub out their original answer and draw a line under their new choice.

In this booklet, there are four different sorts of questions for you to answer.

Turn over and look at the first questions. In every line of words, there is a general word and five examples of it. You have to find the general word and then draw a line under it.

We're going to do the first one together.

Let's read it – ***sense smell touch sight hearing taste****.*

*The general word is '****sense****' and* ***smell, touch, sight, hearing*** *and* ***taste*** *are all examples of our senses. Draw a line under '****sense****'.*

Check that the pupils have understood what they have to do.

Answer the questions on this page and the next page in the same way, and then wait until I tell you to turn over.

Check that the pupils have completed the two pages.

Turn over and look at the next set of questions. In each question, there is a word printed in ***bold****, followed by four words in brackets. You have to find the word in brackets that is most similar in meaning to the word in* ***bold****, and then draw a line under that word.*

Let's look at the first one together.

The word in bold is ***anxiety*** *and the words in brackets are* ***pulse nerves worry calm****. The most similar word to* ***anxiety*** *is* ***worry****. So draw a line under* ***worry****.*

Check that the pupils have understood what they have to do.

Answer the rest of the questions on this page in the same way.

Check that the pupils have completed the page.

Let's look at the next page. In each question there is a word followed by four pictures. You have to find the picture that illustrates the word, and then draw a line under the picture you have chosen.

Look at the first word ***carnivorous****. Which picture shows a carnivorous animal? It's the tyrannosaurus, picture* ***B****, so draw a line under that picture.*

Check that the pupils have understood what they have to do.

Answer the rest of the questions on this page in the same way, and then wait until I tell you to turn over.

Check that the pupils have completed the page.

Turn over and look at the questions on the next page. There are some sentences printed in ***bold*** *which have four other sentences underneath them. You have to read the sentences and then draw a line under the only sentence that you can be* ***sure*** *is true.*

Look at the first sentences in bold.
Salim is going to work to become a chef. To become a chef you have to train for three years.

Now let's read the four sentences underneath.
Salim has decided it takes too long to become a chef.
Salim is going to train for three years.
Salim is already a good cook.
Salim's Dad cooks for him at home.

The first sentence in bold tells us that Salim wants to become a chef and the second sentence tells us that a chef's training takes three years. Therefore Salim is going to train for three years, making sentence ***B*** *the right answer. So draw a line under sentence* ***B*** *.*

Check that the pupils have understood what they have to do.

Now answer the rest of the questions in the booklet in the same way.

Check that the pupils have completed the test and then collect in the booklets for marking.

Group size
The test is designed to be administered to whole classes or large groups. If you wish, you may vary this, depending on the independence of the pupils concerned, testing in small groups or individually, as appropriate.

Timing
No time limit is set for the test, but most pupils will complete it within 30–40 minutes. However, the pupils should not be given a strict time limit, but allowed as much time as they need to attempt all the questions.

Preparation
Each pupil will need:

- a copy of the test booklet;
- a pencil.

You will need a copy of the test as well as these instructions.

Test conditions
It is important that the pupils complete their answers without discussion, collaboration or copying. However, if a pupil needs additional explanation in order to understand how to answer the questions, you may give this.

Method of answering
All the questions are answered by drawing a line under the chosen answer. If the pupils you are working with are used to indicating their answers by some other means (for example, by drawing a ring round their chosen answer) rather than by underlining, they may answer in this way. The instructions you give the pupils will need to be modified accordingly.

Answers may be altered by rubbing or crossing out.

Question numbers
The pupils' test booklets contain question numbers. These are included to make marking easier. You should not refer pupils to them when working through the test.

Giving the test
Suggested wording for you to use when explaining the questions is given in *italics*. You do not need to keep to this verbatim – the most important thing is that the pupils know what they have to do. As you introduce each new section, pause to give them time to read through the printed instructions before you start working through the practice example.

Be as encouraging as possible, but do not give feedback as to whether answers are right or wrong.

Give each pupil a copy of the test booklet.

Ask the pupils to write their name in the appropriate place. (If you wish, the pupils can continue to fill in the required details, or an adult can complete these.) Explain how the pupils are to answer the questions – by drawing a line under the answer they have chosen. If they wish to change an answer, they should cross or rub out their original answer and draw a line under their new choice.

In this booklet, there are four different sorts of questions for you to answer.

Look at the question on the first page. Here you have to find a 'partner' for the shape or pattern in a box by itself.

We're going to do the first one all together.

Look at the two sets of shapes in the first box and decide how they go together. Then look at the third set of shapes, in a box by itself. Which of the five sets of shapes on the right goes with the set of shapes on its own to make a pair, in the same way as the first two sets? Draw a line under the set of shapes that makes a pair in the same way as the first two sets.

*The answer is the first set, set **A**. In the first box, there is a one purple square above and one purple square below a diagonal line followed by one purple triangle above and two purple triangles below a diagonal line. The set of shapes in the box by itself is one purple hexagon above and one purple hexagon below a diagonal line, so its partner must be the first set, set **A**, with one purple pentagon above and two purple pentagons below a diagonal line. So draw a line under set **A**.*

Check that the pupils have understood what they have to do.

Turn over and answer the questions on the next two pages in the same way, and then wait until I tell you to turn over.

Check that all the pupils have completed the two pages.

Turn over and look at the next page. Here you have to find the shape in each question that fits into the space with a question mark.

We're going to do the first one all together.

Look at the top row of boxes. Four of the boxes have shapes in them and one has a question mark. The shapes in the boxes follow a sequence. Look at the shapes on the right and decide which one should go in the box with a question mark. Then draw a line under that shape.

*In the first box, there is a white star with three points, then in the second box there is a purple diamond. In the fourth box, there is a purple pentagon and in the last box a white star with five points. The missing shape is the white star with four points, shape **A**. So draw a line under shape **A**.*

Check that the pupils have understood what they have to do.

Answer the rest of the questions on this page and the next page in the same way, and then wait until I tell you to turn over.

Check that all the pupils have completed these pages.

Turn over and look at the questions on the next page. There are sequences of four numbers, followed by a question mark. There are then a further four numbers and you have to work out which of these comes next in the sequence.

*Look at the first one – **32, 16, 8, 4**. Which number comes next? **6, 0, 2** or **1**?*

*The sequence **32, 16, 8, 4** follows a rule. You have to discover the rule and then work out which number comes next.*

In this case the number is divided by 2 each time. 32 divided by 2 equals 16, 16 divided by 2 equals 8, 8 divided by 2 equals 4, and 4 divided by 2 equals 2, so you should draw a line under the number 2.

For each question, you need to work out the rule – it will not always be 'divide by 2'.

Check that the pupils have understood what they have to do.

Answer the rest of the questions on this page in the same way.

Check that all the pupils have completed the questions.

Now look at the questions on the next page. There are some patterns for you to look at. Each pattern in the boxes on the left has a question mark to show where a piece of the pattern is missing. You have to look at the shapes on the right to find the missing piece and draw a line under it.

We're going to do the first one together.

*Look at the pattern in the first box on the left. There is a piece missing from the pattern. Look at the patterns on the right. Which one is the missing piece? The answer is the last piece, piece **E**, because that completes the pattern of the lines. So draw a line under piece **E**.*

Check that the pupils have understood what they have to do.

Now answer the rest of the questions in this booklet in the same way. Make sure that you turn over and answer the questions on the back cover.

Check that the pupils have completed the test and then collect in the booklets for marking.

Ignore the practice questions when you are marking the tests. Award one mark for each correct answer. No marks should be awarded for multiple-choice questions where more than one choice has been selected. Do not award half-marks.

1. LIT
   STONE*
2. RIDE
   PRAISE*
3. EAT
   BRAKE*
4. SIGHT
   PLAN*
5. LIP
   CAMP*
6. TREE
   HANGER*
7. CARER
   BREATHE*
8. fingers
9. pencil
10. smooth
11. plant
12. four
13. farm
14. pair
15. dome
16. beat
17. wait
18. tear
19. male
20. share
21. B
22. C
23. B
24. B
25. sound
26. utensil
27. period
28. County
29. light

* For questions marked with an asterisk, only award a mark if both answers are correct.

Ignore the practice questions when you are marking the tests. Award one mark for each correct answer. No marks should be awarded for multiple-choice questions where more than one choice has been selected. Do not award half-marks.

1. E
2. D
3. C
4. E
5. E
6. D
7. A
8. C
9. E
10. B
11. D
12. C
13. C
14. B
15. A
16. C
17. E
18. D
19. A
20. A
21. B
22. B
23. D
24. B
25. A
26. D
27. A
28. A
29. A
30. C
31. D
32. E

Marking — Verbal Test 4

Ignore the practice questions when you are marking the tests. Award one mark for each correct answer. No marks should be awarded for multiple-choice questions where more than one choice has been selected. Do not award half-marks.

1. parachute
2. saucepan
3. goldfish
4. owl
5. soft
6. beach
7. texture
8. pencil
9. knee
10. vast
11. undertake
12. D
13. C
14. A
15. B
16. CASE CHORE*
17. PAY LATE*
18. STAR STRIPE*
19. BUSH CRASH*
20. RAIN DAIRY*
21. STEM LAID*
22. OTHER BOLD*
23. STAR CANE*
24. solid
25. top
26. river
27. sons
28. light
29. greet
30. poetry music*

* For questions marked with an asterisk, only award a mark if both answers are correct.

Ignore the practice questions when you are marking the tests. Award one mark for each correct answer. No marks should be awarded for multiple-choice questions where more than one choice has been selected. Do not award half-marks.

1. E
2. E
3. C
4. B
5. A
6. E
7. A
8. C
9. B
10. D
11. D
12. E
13. E
14. A
15. E
16. B
17. C
18. C
19. 18
20. 50
21. 7
22. 4
23. 8
24. 109
25. 9
26. 52
27. 250
28. C
29. E
30. E
31. B
32. E
33. B

Marking Verbal Test 5

Ignore the practice questions when you are marking the tests. Award one mark for each correct answer. No marks should be awarded for multiple-choice questions where more than one choice has been selected. Do not award half-marks.

1. D
2. D
3. C
4. C

5. excavate
6. depend
7. old
8. confidential
9. horrified
10. same

11. sit
12. can
13. lop

14. milk
15. sky
16. plastic
17. plural
18. Cold hot*
19. Sailing flying*
20. Skin fur*
21. angry calm*
22. tadpole caterpillar*
23. hearing seeing*

24. D
25. D

26. C
27. B
28. B
29. D
30. A

* For questions marked with an asterisk, only award a mark if both answers are correct.

Ignore the practice questions when you are marking the tests. Award one mark for each correct answer. No marks should be awarded for multiple-choice questions where more than one choice has been selected. Do not award half-marks.

1. D
2. D
3. C
4. D
5. A
6. A
7. D
8. C
9. D
10. E
11. A
12. B
13. C
14. D
15. E
16. E
17. B
18. A
19. B
20. E
21. 5
22. 20
23. 18
24. 25
25. 15
26. 84
27. 16
28. 26
29. 45
30. 32
31. D
32. D
33. C
34. A
35. E

Ignore the practice questions when you are marking the tests. Award one mark for each correct answer. No marks should be awarded for multiple-choice questions where more than one choice has been selected. Do not award half-marks.

1. sensation
2. cover
3. mood
4. Mountains
5. herb
6. art

7. non-fiction
8. fastening
9. poetry
10. heat

11. pretend
12. permit
13. understand
14. border
15. balance
16. cautious
17. shorten
18. full
19. question

20. A
21. C
22. C
23. C

24. D
25. A

26. A
27. D
28. B
29. A
30. D
31. B

Ignore the practice questions when you are marking the tests. Award one mark for each correct answer. No marks should be awarded for multiple-choice questions where more than one choice has been selected. Do not award half-marks.

1. E
2. B
3. E
4. D
5. D
6. A
7. B
8. E
9. B
10. D
11. A
12. B
13. D
14. C
15. B
16. D
17. E
18. B
19. B
20. E
21. D
22. A
23. A
24. E
25. 90
26. 1/
27. 38
28. 0.4
29. 46
30. 105
31. 30
32. 39
33. 17
34. 2880
35. A
36. A
37. A
38. C

Using and interpreting the conversion tables

Standardised scores

Once you have marked a test, the tables in this manual allow you to convert each pupil's 'raw score' (ie the number of questions correctly answered) into the following forms:

- standardised scores – see pages 42–9;
- expected national curriculum levels – see pages 50–3.

To obtain standardised scores, you will need to work out each pupil's chronological age, in years and completed months, at the date of test. From this, a percentile score can also be obtained – see the table below.

A standardised score can be obtained by following these steps:

- read down the raw-score column at the left or right sides of the conversion table to the row which gives the pupil's raw score;
- read along the row until the column which corresponds with the pupil's chronological age in years and completed months is reached;
- the number at this intersection is the standardised score for a pupil of that chronological age and raw-score level.

Standardised scores are on a normative scale with a mean of 100 – ie the closer a score is to 100, the closer the pupil is to the average or norm for their age group. Approximately 34 per cent of pupils in a group typical of their age will earn standardised scores between 100 and 115, and a further 34 per cent will score in the 85 to 100 range. (This does not mean that you should necessarily expect the same pattern of scores in your own school or class, however.) So, for example, a score of 94 would be somewhat below average, but not greatly so. A standardised score of 120, on the other hand, would place a pupil in the top 10 per cent for their age in terms of verbal or nonverbal ability.

Performance on reasoning tests is to some extent dependent on chronological age: older pupils tend to be better at such tests. The standardised score tables for *Verbal* and *Nonverbal Tests 3–6* thus incorporate an adjustment for differences in test performance which are attributable to differences in chronological age. Thus a pupil whose raw score earns a standardised score of 100 (the mean) can be considered average only in relation to other pupils of the same chronological age in years and completed months. The same raw score would be above average for younger pupils and below average if they were older.

The adjustment for maturity incorporated in the standardised score tables can be helpful in considering the relative ability of pupils of different ages; for example, the very youngest pupils in class might otherwise be too readily judged to have a lower reasoning ability than 'expected'.

Percentile equivalents are:

Standardised score:	70	75	80	85	90	95	100	105	110	115	120	125	130
Percentile:	2	5	9	16	26	37	50	63	74	84	91	95	98

Relating reasoning ability to educational attainment

The *Reasoning Progress Tests* can be used to compare a pupil's actual attainment with the level you might expect, given their ability. This can be done on a broad impression basis: where a pupil does not, in the teacher's view, seem to be fulfilling his or her potential, the tests will help to probe this possibility further; conversely, pupils who score highly on the tests but are not performing well in curriculum subjects may be singled out for closer investigation.

More systematic comparisons can be made by reference to the pupil's standardised scores on published attainment tests, such as the *Reading Progress Tests* series, the *Numeracy Progress Tests* series and the *Hodder Group Reading Tests*. Generally, there should be some consistency between pupils' standardised scores as measured by these and other published attainment tests, and the *Reasoning Progress Tests*. Where reasoning ability scores exceed attainment scores, this may be indicative that a child is underachieving.

At the same time, *precise* concordance between scores should not be expected. Tests standardised with different samples of pupils in different years and at different times of year will not be directly comparable. However, within a given class or year group, pupils who perform poorly on attainment tests, compared to their peers, but achieve a much higher ranking on a reasoning test will be candidates for further investigation. How big does a difference between ability and attainment have to be to mean a child is underachieving? A precise, reliable threshold figure which would have universal validity cannot be given to indicate that a child's attainment is *genuinely* below their ability. However, differences of 15 points or more are likely to be of serious concern and differences of 5 points or less are unlikely to be serious grounds for concern.Those pupils with the greatest discrepancy between standardised scores for reasoning and attainment will be of the highest priority. Moreover, the expression of the difference in standardised score terms can make it easier to convey the magnitude of the problem to parents, teachers and other professionals.

National curriculum levels

Validity research conducted during the development of the tests (see pages 56–7) found a positive relationship between reasoning ability and attainment on national curriculum tests. This relationship varied depending upon the criterion of national curriculum attainment which was used, but some broad norms emerged and these were used to create expectancy tables (pages 50–3) which can be used to show, at a very general level, whether pupils are achieving the national curriculum levels to be expected given their ability, or whether they are doing better or less well than their ability would suggest.

The tables are based on the statistical correlation between reasoning ability and national curriculum test results in a complete sample of pupils across year groups 2 to 6. This means that purely 'theoretical' national curriculum levels can be estimated for some reasoning tests. For this reason, the upper sections of some tables contain asterisks rather than national curriculum levels. This means that the level of reasoning ability the pupil has exhibited is consistent with a level of national curriculum attainment as high as or possibly higher than the final (ie preceding) level actually tabulated.

Verbal Test 3 conversion table

raw score	chronological age in years and completed months										raw score
	6:11 - 7:1	7:2- 7:4	7:5- 7:7	7:8- 7:10	7:11- 8:1	8:2- 8:4	8:5- 8:7	8:8- 8:10	8:11 - 9:1	9:2- 9:4	
1	70-	70-	70-	70-	70-	70-	70-	70-	70-	70-	*1*
2	72	71	70-	70-	70-	70-	70-	70-	70-	70-	*2*
3	77	76	75	74	72	71	70	70-	70-	70-	*3*
4	82	81	80	79	78	76	75	74	73	72	*4*
5	84	83	82	81	80	79	78	76	75	74	*5*
6	87	86	85	84	82	81	80	79	78	77	*6*
7	90	88	87	86	85	84	83	81	80	79	*7*
8	92	91	90	89	88	86	85	84	83	82	*8*
9	94	92	91	90	89	88	86	85	84	83	*9*
10	96	95	94	93	91	90	89	88	87	86	*10*
11	98	96	95	94	93	92	90	89	88	87	*11*
12	100	99	98	97	95	94	93	92	91	89	*12*
13	102	100	99	98	97	96	94	93	92	91	*13*
14	103	102	101	99	98	97	96	94	93	92	*14*
15	106	105	103	102	101	100	98	97	96	95	*15*
16	107	106	105	104	102	101	100	99	97	96	*16*
17	109	108	106	105	104	102	101	100	99	97	*17*
18	112	111	109	108	107	105	104	103	102	100	*18*
19	113	112	111	109	108	107	106	104	103	102	*19*
20	116	115	114	112	111	110	109	107	106	105	*20*
21	118	116	115	114	113	111	110	109	107	106	*21*
22	121	119	118	117	115	114	113	112	110	109	*22*
23	123	122	121	120	118	117	116	114	113	112	*23*
24	126	125	123	122	121	120	118	117	116	115	*24*
25	128	127	126	125	123	122	121	120	119	117	*25*
26	132	131	130	129	128	127	126	125	123	122	*26*
27	136	135	134	133	132	131	130	129	128	127	*27*
28	140+	140+	140	139	138	138	137	136	135	134	*28*

Nonverbal Test 3 conversion table

raw score	chronological age in years and completed months 6:11 - 7:1	7:2- 7:4	7:5- 7:7	7:8- 7:10	7:11- 8:1	8:2- 8:4	8:5- 8:7	8:8- 8:10	8:11 - 9:1	9:2- 9:4	raw score
4	75	73	72	71	70-	70-	70-	70-	70-	70-	4
5	78	77	76	75	74	72	71	70	70-	70-	5
6	82	81	80	79	77	76	75	74	73	72	6
7	84	83	82	81	80	79	78	76	75	74	7
8	87	86	85	83	82	81	80	79	78	77	8
9	89	88	87	86	85	84	83	81	80	79	9
10	92	91	90	89	87	86	85	84	83	82	10
11	95	94	92	91	90	89	88	86	85	84	11
12	97	96	95	94	93	91	90	89	88	87	12
13	99	98	96	95	94	93	92	90	89	88	13
14	101	100	99	98	97	95	94	93	92	91	14
15	104	103	102	101	99	98	97	96	94	93	15
16	106	105	103	102	101	99	98	97	96	95	16
17	109	107	106	105	104	102	101	100	99	97	17
18	110	109	108	106	105	104	102	101	100	99	18
19	113	112	111	109	108	107	105	104	103	102	19
20	115	113	112	111	109	108	107	106	104	103	20
21	118	116	115	114	112	111	110	109	107	106	21
22	121	119	118	117	115	114	113	111	110	109	22
23	123	122	121	120	118	117	115	114	113	112	23
24	126	125	123	122	121	120	118	117	116	114	24
25	128	127	126	125	123	122	121	120	118	117	25
26	130	129	128	127	126	125	123	122	121	120	26
27	132	131	130	129	128	127	126	125	123	122	27
28	135	134	133	132	131	130	129	128	127	126	28
29	138	137	137	136	135	135	134	133	132	131	29
30	140+	140+	140+	140+	140+	139	139	138	137	136	30
31	140+	140+	140+	140+	140+	140+	140+	140+	140+	140+	31

Verbal Test 4 conversion table

raw score	chronological age in years and completed months 7:11 - 8:1	8:2- 8:4	8:5- 8:7	8:8- 8:10	8:11 - 9:1	9:2- 9:4	9:5- 9:7	9:8- 9:10	9:11- 10:1	10:2- 10:4	raw score
1	70-	70-	70-	70-	70-	70-	70-	70-	70-	70-	1
2	74	73	71	70	70-	70-	70-	70-	70-	70-	2
3	79	78	76	75	74	73	72	71	70-	70-	3
4	82	81	80	79	78	77	75	74	73	72	4
5	85	84	83	81	80	79	78	77	76	74	5
6	88	86	85	84	83	82	80	79	78	77	6
7	90	89	88	87	85	84	83	82	81	79	7
8	93	92	90	89	88	87	86	84	83	82	8
9	94	93	92	91	89	88	87	86	85	83	9
10	97	96	94	93	92	91	90	88	87	86	10
11	98	97	96	94	93	92	91	90	89	87	11
12	101	100	98	97	96	95	94	92	91	90	12
13	102	101	100	99	97	96	95	94	93	91	13
14	104	102	101	100	99	97	96	95	94	93	14
15	107	105	104	103	102	100	99	98	97	95	15
16	108	107	106	104	103	102	100	99	98	97	16
17	110	108	107	106	105	103	102	101	99	98	17
18	111	110	109	107	106	105	103	102	101	99	18
19	114	113	111	110	109	108	106	105	104	102	19
20	115	114	113	112	110	109	108	107	105	104	20
21	118	117	116	114	113	112	111	109	108	107	21
22	120	118	117	116	114	113	112	111	110	108	22
23	122	121	120	118	117	116	115	114	112	111	23
24	125	123	122	121	120	119	117	116	115	114	24
25	127	126	125	123	122	121	120	119	118	116	25
26	129	128	127	126	124	123	122	121	120	119	26
27	132	131	130	129	128	127	126	124	123	122	27
28	137	137	136	135	134	133	132	131	129	128	28
29	140+	140+	140+	140+	140+	140	139	138	138	137	29

Nonverbal Test 4 conversion table

raw score	chronological age in years and completed months										raw score
	7:11 - 8:1	**8:2- 8:4**	**8:5- 8:7**	**8:8- 8:10**	**8:11 - 9:1**	**9:2- 9:4**	**9:5- 9:7**	**9:8- 9:10**	**9:11- 10:1**	**10:2- 10:4**	
2	70-	70-	70-	70-	70-	70-	70-	70-	70-	70-	*2*
3	70-	70-	70-	70-	70-	70-	70-	70-	70-	70-	*3*
4	70-	70-	70-	70-	70-	70-	70-	70-	70-	70-	*4*
5	70-	70-	70-	70-	70-	70-	70-	70-	70-	70-	*5*
6	70-	70-	70-	70-	70-	70-	70-	70-	70-	70-	*6*
7	71	70-	70-	70-	70-	70-	70-	70-	70-	70-	*7*
8	74	72	71	70	70-	70-	70-	70-	70-	70-	*8*
9	75	74	73	71	70	70-	70-	70-	70-	70-	*9*
10	77	76	75	74	73	72	70	70-	70-	70-	*10*
11	79	78	76	75	74	73	72	70	70-	70-	*11*
12	81	80	79	78	76	75	74	73	72	71	*12*
13	82	81	80	79	78	77	75	74	73	72	*13*
14	85	84	83	81	80	79	78	77	75	74	*14*
15	86	85	84	83	81	80	79	78	77	76	*15*
16	87	86	85	84	83	82	80	79	78	77	*16*
17	89	88	86	85	84	83	82	80	79	78	*17*
18	91	90	89	88	87	85	84	83	82	81	*18*
19	93	91	90	89	88	87	86	84	83	82	*19*
20	94	93	92	90	89	88	87	86	84	83	*20*
21	97	95	94	93	92	91	89	88	87	86	*21*
22	98	97	96	94	93	92	91	90	88	87	*22*
23	101	99	98	97	96	95	93	92	91	90	*23*
24	102	101	100	98	97	96	95	94	92	91	*24*
25	105	104	102	101	100	99	97	96	95	94	*25*
26	108	107	105	104	103	102	100	99	98	97	*26*
27	111	110	108	107	106	105	103	102	101	99	*27*
28	114	113	111	110	109	107	106	105	104	102	*28*
29	117	115	114	113	112	110	109	108	107	105	*29*
30	122	121	120	118	117	116	115	113	112	111	*30*
31	127	126	125	123	122	121	120	119	117	116	*31*
32	134	133	133	132	130	129	128	127	126	124	*32*

Verbal Test 5 conversion table

raw score	chronological age in years and completed months 8:11 - 9:1	9:2-9:4	9:5-9:7	9:8-9:10	9:11-10:1	10:2-10:4	10:5-10:7	10:8-10:10	10:11 - 11:1	11:2-11:4	raw score
1	70-	70-	70-	70-	70-	70-	70-	70-	70-	70-	*1*
2	70	70-	70-	70-	70-	70-	70-	70-	70-	70-	*2*
3	75	74	73	72	71	70-	70-	70-	70-	70-	*3*
4	79	78	77	75	74	73	72	71	70-	70-	*4*
5	83	82	80	79	78	77	76	74	73	72	*5*
6	85	84	83	82	81	79	78	77	76	75	*6*
7	88	87	86	84	83	82	81	79	78	77	*7*
8	91	89	88	87	86	85	83	82	81	80	*8*
9	92	91	90	88	87	86	85	84	82	81	*9*
10	95	93	92	91	90	89	88	86	85	84	*10*
11	96	95	94	92	91	90	89	88	86	85	*11*
12	99	97	96	95	94	93	91	90	89	88	*12*
13	100	99	98	96	95	94	93	92	90	89	*13*
14	102	100	99	98	97	95	94	93	92	91	*14*
15	105	103	102	101	99	98	97	96	94	93	*15*
16	106	105	103	102	101	99	98	97	96	95	*16*
17	107	106	105	104	102	101	100	98	97	96	*17*
18	110	109	108	107	105	104	103	101	100	99	*18*
19	112	111	109	108	107	105	104	103	101	100	*19*
20	113	112	111	109	108	107	106	104	103	102	*20*
21	116	115	113	112	111	110	109	107	106	105	*21*
22	117	116	115	114	112	111	110	109	107	106	*22*
23	120	119	117	116	115	114	113	111	110	109	*23*
24	122	121	120	119	118	116	115	114	113	112	*24*
25	124	123	122	121	120	119	118	117	115	114	*25*
26	128	127	126	124	123	122	121	120	119	118	*26*
27	132	131	129	128	127	126	124	123	122	121	*27*
28	136	136	135	134	132	131	130	128	127	125	*28*
29	140+	140+	140+	140+	140	139	138	137	136	135	*29*

Nonverbal Test 5 conversion table

raw score	chronological age in years and completed months										raw score
	8:11 - 9:1	9:2- 9:4	9:5- 9:7	9:8- 9:10	9:11- 10:1	10:2- 10:4	10:5- 10:7	10:8- 10:10	10:11 - 11:1	11:2- 11:4	
3	70-	70-	70-	70-	70-	70-	70-	70-	70-	70-	3
4	70-	70-	70-	70-	70-	70-	70-	70-	70-	70-	4
5	70-	70-	70-	70-	70-	70-	70-	70-	70-	70-	5
6	70-	70-	70-	70-	70-	70-	70-	70-	70-	70-	6
7	70-	70-	70-	70-	70-	70-	70-	70-	70-	70-	7
8	70-	70-	70-	70-	70-	70-	70-	70-	70-	70-	8
9	70	70-	70-	70-	70-	70-	70-	70-	70-	70-	9
10	73	72	70	70-	70-	70-	70-	70-	70-	70-	10
11	75	74	73	72	71	70-	70-	70-	70-	70-	11
12	76	75	74	73	72	71	70-	70-	70-	70-	12
13	79	78	77	75	74	73	72	71	70-	70-	13
14	80	79	78	77	75	74	73	72	71	70-	14
15	83	82	80	79	78	77	76	74	73	72	15
16	84	83	82	80	79	78	77	76	74	73	16
17	87	85	84	83	82	81	79	78	77	76	17
18	88	87	86	84	83	82	81	79	78	77	18
19	89	88	87	86	84	83	82	81	79	78	19
20	92	91	89	88	87	86	85	83	82	81	20
21	93	92	91	90	88	87	86	85	84	82	21
22	94	93	92	91	90	89	87	86	85	84	22
23	97	96	95	94	92	91	90	89	88	86	23
24	99	97	96	95	94	93	91	90	89	88	24
25	101	100	99	98	96	95	94	93	92	90	25
26	103	102	100	99	98	97	95	94	93	92	26
27	106	105	103	102	101	99	98	97	96	94	27
28	109	107	106	105	104	102	101	100	98	97	28
29	112	110	109	108	107	105	104	103	101	100	29
30	114	113	112	111	109	108	107	106	104	103	30
31	118	117	116	115	114	112	111	110	109	107	31
32	122	121	120	119	117	116	115	114	113	112	32
33	127	126	124	123	122	121	120	119	118	117	33
34	135	134	133	132	131	129	128	127	126	124	34

Verbal Test 6 conversion table

raw score	chronological age in years and completed months										raw score
	9:11 - 10:1	**10:2- 10:4**	**10:5- 10:7**	**10:8- 10:10**	**10:11 - 11:1**	**11:2- 11:4**	**11:5- 11:7**	**11:8- 11:10**	**11:11 - 12:1**	**12:2- 12:4**	
1	70-	70-	70-	70-	70-	70-	70-	70-	70-	70-	*1*
2	70-	70-	70-	70-	70-	70-	70-	70-	70-	70-	*2*
3	73	72	71	70-	70-	70-	70-	70-	70-	70-	*3*
4	77	76	74	73	72	71	70-	70-	70-	70-	*4*
5	81	79	78	77	76	75	73	72	71	70	*5*
6	83	82	81	79	78	77	76	75	74	73	*6*
7	86	85	83	82	81	80	78	77	76	75	*7*
8	89	87	86	85	84	82	81	80	78	77	*8*
9	91	90	89	88	86	85	84	83	81	80	*9*
10	94	93	91	90	89	88	87	85	84	83	*10*
11	95	94	93	92	90	89	88	87	86	84	*11*
12	97	95	94	93	92	91	89	88	87	86	*12*
13	99	98	97	96	94	93	92	91	90	88	*13*
14	101	99	98	97	96	95	93	92	91	90	*14*
15	104	102	101	100	98	97	96	95	94	92	*15*
16	105	104	103	101	100	99	97	96	95	94	*16*
17	107	105	104	103	101	100	99	98	96	95	*17*
18	110	108	107	106	104	103	102	100	99	98	*18*
19	111	110	109	107	106	105	103	102	101	99	*19*
20	112	111	110	109	107	106	105	103	102	101	*20*
21	115	114	113	111	110	109	108	107	105	104	*21*
22	116	115	114	113	112	110	109	108	107	105	*22*
23	119	118	116	115	114	113	112	111	110	108	*23*
24	121	120	119	118	117	115	114	113	112	111	*24*
25	122	121	120	119	118	117	116	114	113	112	*25*
26	126	124	123	122	121	120	119	118	117	116	*26*
27	128	127	126	124	123	122	121	120	119	118	*27*
28	132	131	130	128	127	125	124	123	122	121	*28*
29	138	137	136	134	133	132	130	129	127	125	*29*
30	140+	140+	140+	140+	140+	140+	139+	138+	137+	136+	*30*

Nonverbal Test 6 conversion table

raw score	chronological age in years and completed months: 9:11 - 10:1	10:2- 10:4	10:5- 10:7	10:8- 10:10	10:11 - 11:1	11:2- 11:4	11:5- 11:7	11:8- 11:10	11:11 - 12:1	12:2- 12:4	*raw score*
1	70-	70-	70-	70-	70-	70-	70-	70-	70-	70-	*1*
2	70-	70-	70-	70-	70-	70-	70-	70-	70-	70-	*2*
3	70-	70-	70-	70-	70-	70-	70-	70-	70-	70-	*3*
4	70-	70-	70-	70-	70-	70-	70-	70-	70-	70-	*4*
5	70-	70-	70-	70-	70-	70-	70-	70-	70-	70-	*5*
6	70-	70-	70-	70-	70-	70-	70-	70-	70-	70-	*6*
7	71	70-	70-	70-	70-	70-	70-	70-	70-	70-	*7*
8	73	72	71	70-	70-	70-	70-	70-	70-	70-	*8*
9	75	74	73	72	71	70-	70-	70-	70-	70-	*9*
10	77	76	74	73	72	71	70-	70-	70-	70-	*10*
11	79	78	77	76	74	73	72	71	70	70-	*11*
12	80	79	78	77	76	75	73	72	71	70	*12*
13	82	81	79	78	77	76	75	73	72	71	*13*
14	84	83	82	81	79	78	77	76	75	74	*14*
15	86	85	83	82	81	79	78	77	76	75	*15*
16	87	86	85	83	82	81	80	78	77	76	*16*
17	88	87	86	85	84	82	81	80	78	77	*17*
18	91	90	89	88	86	85	84	82	81	80	*18*
19	92	91	90	89	88	86	85	84	83	81	*19*
20	94	93	91	90	89	88	87	85	84	83	*20*
21	95	94	93	91	90	89	88	87	85	84	*21*
22	96	95	94	93	92	90	89	88	87	86	*22*
23	98	97	95	94	93	92	91	89	88	87	*23*
24	101	99	98	97	96	94	93	92	91	90	*24*
25	102	101	99	98	97	96	95	93	92	91	*25*
26	104	102	101	100	98	97	96	95	93	92	*26*
27	105	104	102	101	100	98	97	96	95	94	*27*
28	108	107	105	104	103	101	100	99	98	96	*28*
29	109	108	107	106	104	103	102	100	99	98	*29*
30	112	111	110	109	107	106	105	103	102	101	*30*
31	114	112	111	110	109	107	106	105	103	102	*31*
32	116	115	114	113	111	110	109	108	107	105	*32*
33	120	119	118	116	115	114	113	112	111	110	*33*
34	122	121	120	119	118	117	115	114	113	112	*34*
35	126	124	123	122	121	120	119	118	117	116	*35*
36	131	129	128	127	126	124	123	122	121	120	*36*
37	140	139	138	137	136	135	134	132	131	129	*37*

Expected national curriculum levels

Verbal Test 3

Raw Score	English Level	Reading Level	Writing Level	Spelling Level	Maths Level
1	1	1	1	1	1
2	1	1	1	1	1
3	1	1	1	1	2
4	1	2	2	1	2
5	2	2	2	1	2
6	2	2	2	2	2
7	2	2	2	2	2
8	2	2	2	2	2
9	2	2	2	2	2
10	2	2	2	2	2
11	2	3	2	2	3
12	2	3	2	2	3
13	2	3	2	2	3
14	3	3	2	2	3
15	3	3	3	2	3
16	3	3	3	2	3
17	3	3	3	2	3
18	3	3	3	3	3
19	3	3	3	3	3
20	3	3	3	3	3
21	3	3	3	3	3
22	3	3	3	3	3
23	3	4	3	3	4
24	4	4	3	3	4
25	4	4	3	3	4
26	4	4	3	3	4
27	4	4	4	3	4
28+	*	*	4	4	*

Nonverbal Test 3

Raw Score	English Level	Reading Level	Writing Level	Spelling Level	Maths Level
2	1	1	1	1	1
3	2	2	2	1	2
4	2	2	2	2	2
5	2	2	2	2	2
6	2	2	2	2	2
7	2	2	2	2	2
8	2	3	2	2	2
9	2	3	2	2	3
10	3	3	2	2	3
11	3	3	2	2	3
12	3	3	3	2	3
13	3	3	3	2	3
14	3	3	3	3	3
15	3	3	3	3	3
16	3	3	3	3	3
17	3	3	3	3	3
18	3	3	3	3	3
19	3	4	3	3	4
20	3	4	3	3	4
21	4	4	3	3	4
22	4	4	3	3	4
23	4	4	3	3	4
24	4	4	3	3	4
25	4	4	3	3	4
26	4	4	4	3	4
27	4	4	4	4	4
28	4	4	4	4	*
29	*	*	4	4	*
30	*	*	4	4	*
31+	*	*	4	4	*

Expected national curriculum levels

Verbal Test 4

Raw Score	English Level	Reading Level	Writing Level	Spelling Level	Maths Level
1	1	1	1	1	1
2	1	2	2	1	2
3	2	2	2	2	2
4	2	2	2	2	2
5	2	2	2	2	2
6	2	2	2	2	2
7	2	2	2	2	2
8	2	3	2	2	3
9	2	3	2	2	3
10	2	3	2	2	3
11	3	3	2	2	3
12	3	3	3	2	3
13	3	3	3	2	3
14	3	3	3	2	3
15	3	3	3	3	3
16	3	3	3	3	3
17	3	3	3	3	3
18	3	3	3	3	3
19	3	3	3	3	3
20	3	3	3	3	3
21	3	4	3	3	4
22	4	4	3	3	4
23	4	4	3	3	4
24	4	4	3	3	4
25	4	4	3	3	4
26	4	4	3	3	4
27	4	4	4	3	4
28	*	*	4	4	*
29+	*	*	4	4	*

Nonverbal Test 4

Raw Score	English Level	Reading Level	Writing Level	Spelling Level	Maths Level
2	1	1	1	1	1
3	1	1	1	1	1
4	1	2	2	1	1
5	2	2	2	1	2
6	2	2	2	2	2
7	2	2	2	2	2
8	2	2	2	2	2
9	2	2	2	2	2
10	2	2	2	2	2
11	2	2	2	2	2
12	2	2	2	2	2
13	2	3	2	2	2
14	2	3	2	2	3
15	3	3	2	2	3
16	3	3	2	2	3
17	3	3	2	2	3
18	3	3	3	2	3
19	3	3	3	2	3
20	3	3	3	2	3
21	3	3	3	3	3
22	3	3	3	3	3
23	3	3	3	3	3
24	3	3	3	3	3
25	3	3	3	3	3
26	3	4	3	3	4
27	3	4	3	3	4
28	4	4	3	3	4
29	4	4	3	3	4
30	4	4	3	3	4
31	4	4	4	4	4
32+	*	*	4	4	*

Expected national curriculum levels

Verbal Test 5

Raw Score	English Level	Reading Level	Writing Level	Spelling Level	Maths Level
1	1	1	1	1	1
2	1	2	2	1	2
3	2	2	2	1	2
4	2	2	2	2	2
5	2	2	2	2	2
6	2	2	2	2	2
7	2	3	2	2	3
8	2	3	2	2	3
9	2	3	2	2	3
10	3	3	2	2	3
11	3	3	3	2	3
12	3	3	3	2	3
13	3	3	3	2	3
14	3	3	3	3	3
15	3	3	3	3	3
16	3	3	3	3	3
17	3	3	3	3	3
18	3	3	3	3	3
19	3	4	3	3	4
20	3	4	3	3	4
21	4	4	3	3	4
22	4	4	3	3	4
23	4	4	3	3	4
24	4	4	3	3	4
25	4	4	3	3	4
26	4	4	4	3	4
27	4	4	4	4	4
28	5	5	4	4	5
29+	*	*	4	4	*

Nonverbal Test 5

Raw Score	English Level	Reading Level	Writing Level	Spelling Level	Maths Level
3	1	1	1	1	1
4	1	1	1	1	1
5	1	2	2	1	1
6	2	2	2	1	2
7	2	2	2	2	2
8	2	2	2	2	2
9	2	2	2	2	2
10	2	2	2	2	2
11	2	2	2	2	2
12	2	2	2	2	2
13	2	3	2	2	3
14	2	3	2	2	3
15	3	3	2	2	3
16	3	3	2	2	3
17	3	3	3	2	3
18	3	3	3	2	3
19	3	3	3	2	3
20	3	3	3	3	3
21	3	3	3	3	3
22	3	3	3	3	3
23	3	3	3	3	3
24	3	3	3	3	3
25	3	3	3	3	4
26	3	4	3	3	4
27	3	4	3	3	4
28	4	4	3	3	4
29	4	4	3	3	4
30	4	4	3	3	4
31	4	4	3	3	4
32	4	4	4	4	4
33	4	4	4	4	5
34+	5	5	4	4	5

Expected national curriculum levels

Verbal Test 6

Raw Score	English Level	Reading Level	Writing Level	Spelling Level	Maths Level	Science Level
1	1	1	1	1	1	2
2	1	2	2	1	2	2
3	2	2	2	2	2	3
4	2	2	2	2	2	3
5	2	2	2	2	2	3
6	2	3	2	2	3	3
7	2	3	2	2	3	3
8	3	3	2	2	3	3
9	3	3	3	2	3	3
10	3	3	3	2	3	3
11	3	3	3	2	3	3
12	3	3	3	3	3	4
13	3	3	3	3	3	4
14	3	3	3	3	3	4
15	3	3	3	3	3	4
16	3	3	3	3	3	4
17	3	4	3	3	4	4
18	4	4	3	3	4	4
19	4	4	3	3	4	4
20	4	4	3	3	4	4
21	4	4	3	3	4	4
22	4	4	3	3	4	4
23	4	4	3	3	4	4
24	4	4	3	3	4	4
25	4	4	4	3	4	4
26	4	4	4	4	4	5
27	4	5	4	4	4	5
28	5	5	4	4	5	5
29	5	6	4	4	5	6
30+	6	6	5	4	6	6

Nonverbal Test 6

Raw Score	English Level	Reading Level	Writing Level	Spelling Level	Maths Level	Science Level
2	1	1	1	1	1	3
3	2	2	2	1	2	3
4	2	2	2	2	2	3
5	2	2	2	2	2	3
6	2	2	2	2	2	3
7	2	2	2	2	2	3
8	2	3	2	2	2	3
9	2	3	2	2	3	3
10	3	3	2	2	3	3
11	3	3	2	2	3	3
12	3	3	2	2	3	4
13	3	3	3	2	3	4
14	3	3	3	2	3	4
15	3	3	3	3	3	4
16	3	3	3	3	3	4
17	3	3	3	3	3	4
18	3	3	3	3	3	4
19	3	3	3	3	3	4
20	3	3	3	3	3	4
21	3	3	3	3	3	4
22	3	3	3	3	4	4
23	3	4	3	3	4	4
24	3	4	3	3	4	4
25	4	4	3	3	4	4
26	4	4	3	3	4	4
27	4	4	3	3	4	4
28	4	4	3	3	4	4
29	4	4	3	3	4	4
30	4	4	3	3	4	4
31	4	4	3	3	4	4
32	4	4	4	3	4	4
33	4	4	4	4	5	5
34	4	4	4	4	5	5
35	5	5	4	4	5	5
36	5	5	4	4	6	5
37+	6	6	4	4	6	6

Design, construction and standardisation

The types of question used in the *Reasoning Progress Tests* are a representative cross-section of techniques used in existing tests of reasoning for primary and early secondary aged pupils. At the start of the project the development team commissioned a psychologist with experience of working in educational and psychological test publishing to carry out an extensive survey of methods used to test pupils' reasoning ability. From this survey a number of categories were selected and test questions drafted which conformed to these.

A pool of 1100+ questions was assembled for piloting and large-scale standardised trialling between 2000 and 2002. From this, two statistically calibrated sets or 'banks' of test questions were created for respectively, verbal reasoning and nonverbal reasoning. From these banks norms for the ability tested by the questions contained in each bank were derived.

The numbers of pupils whose performance were used for this purpose are as follows:

Test	number of pupils	age range
Verbal ability	6897	5:0 to 13:0
Nonverbal ability	7551	5:0 to 13:0

The published tests were assembled by selecting suitable questions from the bank for each of the intended tests.

Two main considerations guided the selection. First, it was important to ensure that the difficulty of the questions matched the ability range of the age group for which the test was intended. It was also necessary to restrict the types or categories of question to a manageable variety within any one test. As far as possible, the order in which groups of questions occur in any particular test reflects the average difficulty of the group. However, within any one group there is usually a range of easier and harder questions.

Central to the methodology applied to construct the tests is the notion that all questions in a calibrated bank measure a common trait or ability. Rather than setting out to establish age norms for set-piece tests, therefore, this technique of test construction aims to generally estimate age norms for the ability tested by each question in the bank. This relationship between age and ability is assumed to hold good for any selection of questions drawn from the bank.

The standardised score tables were derived by estimating the adjustments needed to take account of the relationship between chronological age and ability for each of the types of test (verbal and nonverbal). Conversion tables for each test were created to give the correspondence between *ability*, based on the difficulty of the items included in each test, and *raw score* so that, for each test, raw scores may be used to apply the standardised score tables.

Validity

Verbal and nonverbal tests containing questions of the kind used in the *Reasoning Progress Tests* would be expected to correlate positively with tests of educational attainment, and indeed other tests of reasoning. To check this was the case, a validity trial was carried out in January and February of 2002. A sample of 57 primary and middle schools trialled two tests of reasoning consisting respectively of 33 verbal questions and 25 nonverbal questions, selected to cover a wide ability range, together with a validity criterion in the form of a published test of attainment or reasoning ability. The attainment tests were taken from the following:

- the *Numeracy Progress Tests* (Denis Vincent and Mary Crumpler, 2000, Hodder & Stoughton)
- the *Reading Progress Tests* (Denis Vincent, Mary Crumpler and Mike de la Mare, 1996, Hodder & Stoughton)
- the *British Spelling Tests* (Denis Vincent and Mary Crumpler, 1997, NFER-NELSON)
- the *Hodder Group Reading Tests* (Denis Vincent and Mary Crumpler, 2000, Hodder & Stoughton).

The *Non-Reading Intelligence Tests* (Dennis Young, 1989, Hodder & Stoughton) were selected as a measure of reasoning ability against which to evaluate the new tests.

In each case, a single class group was tested and the particular version or level of published validity criterion test was selected to match the age range of that class.

Results were returned for 1396 verbal tests and 1394 nonverbal tests for pupils in Year 3 to Year 7 classes and the correlations between the *Reasoning Progress Tests* and the published tests are presented in Table 1 on page 56. Correlation coefficients significant at the 0.01 level or above are printed in boldface. Coefficients that are significant above .05 are printed in normal face and those which failed to reach significance are indicated by 'ns'.

The final column of Table 1 gives multiple correlation coefficients (R) when it was found that by combining the verbal and nonverbal reasoning measures a statistically significantly larger correlation was obtained. For example, although the correlation between verbal reasoning ability and performance on the *British Spelling Test Form 1Y* is higher than that between the spelling test and nonverbal reasoning ability, combining the two measures results in a higher overall multiple correlation. This means that the nonverbal measure added some additional 'power' to the equation which predicts performance on the spelling test. This is consistent with the view that nonverbal tests measure aspects of reasoning ability which are related, in their own right, to academic performance.

The pattern of results is consistent with what might be expected when sampling the relationship between tests in a cross-section of class- or yeargroup-sized samples of children. Generally, reasoning ability is positively related to attainment, but the effect is stronger for verbal reasoning.

Table 1: Correlations (Pearson's *r*) between verbal and nonverbal reasoning ability and published validity criterion tests

Attainment test	Verbal Reasoning correlation coefficient	number of children	Nonverbal Reasoning correlation coefficient	number of children	Multiple R for Verbal and Nonverbal combined
British Spelling Test Series 1X	**0.78**	29	0.47	29	ns
British Spelling Test Series 1Y	**0.46**	102	**0.35**	102	**0.50**
British Spelling Test Series 2X	ns	59	ns	59	ns
British Spelling Test Series 2Y	**0.57**	87	**0.38**	88	ns
British Spelling Test Series 3X	**0.49**	54	**0.54**	54	**0.70**
British Spelling Test Series 3Y	**0.58**	109	**0.40**	109	ns
Hodder Group Reading Test 1A	**0.45**	83	**0.40**	82	**0.53**
Hodder Group Reading Test 1B	ns	24	ns	24	ns
Hodder Group Reading Test 2A	**0.68**	80	**0.40**	80	**0.71**
Hodder Group Reading Test 3A	**0.49**	52	0.27	52	ns
Numeracy Progress Test 3	**0.51**	90	ns	89	ns
Numeracy Progress Test 4	**0.65**	69	**0.51**	69	**0.69**
Numeracy Progress Test 5	**0.55**	96	**0.43**	96	**0.58**
Numeracy Progress Test 6	**0.47**	64	**0.47**	64	**0.57**
Reading Progress Test 3	**0.60**	78	**0.61**	78	**0.69**
Reading Progress Test 4	**0.62**	99	**0.42**	99	**0.67**
Reading Progress Test 5	**0.67**	82	**0.44**	82	ns
Reading Progress Test 6	ns	24	ns	24	ns
Non-Reading Intelligence Test 2	**0.78**	78	**0.60**	77	**0.82**
Non-Reading Intelligence Test 3	**0.69**	37	ns	37	**0.75**

Correlation with national curriculum levels

An important use of the reasoning tests is in considering the performance of children on national curriculum assessments in the light of their performance on the reasoning tests. For this to be a valid application of the tests, it is important to establish that a relationship exists between the ability they measure and national curriculum attainment.

All schools that participated in an early part of the standardisation of the test questions in October and November of 2001 were invited to provide 2002 national curriculum test results for the children who had taken reasoning tests. Results were provided for statutory or non-statutory tests for 916 children from 22 primary schools who had taken verbal tests in 2001 and for 1121 children from 26 primary schools where nonverbal tests had been trialled.

The basis of national curriculum assessments available in 2002 varied somewhat according to the year group and key stage concerned. However, it is common practice to regard a national curriculum level as having the same meaning, regardless of the year group or precise testing technique used to assess it. For the purpose of data analysis this convention was followed wherever feasible, in examining the results of the reasoning tests, so that common scales for national curriculum subjects were applied across year groups.

The reasoning tests had been developed using a statistical model which placed all children on a single ability scale for either verbal or nonverbal reasoning. This was independent of the particular set of test questions they had attempted in the standardisation trials. It was thus possible to derive some quite general measures of the correlation between reasoning ability and national curriculum attainment which reflected cross year-group patterns of agreement.

These correlations between reasoning test ability and all measures of national curriculum attainment were all found to be statistically significant (at above the .01 level) and were usually moderately high, and it should be noted that the national curriculum assessments were based on pupils' performance approximately nine months after they had been tested on reasoning ability. As might be expected, the correlations for the verbal tests were somewhat higher than those for nonverbal reasoning. Table 2 overleaf provides a brief illustration of the results.

Some results for national curriculum tests used age-adjusted standardised scores. However, the figures in Table 2 do not include a corresponding adjustment for age in the reasoning ability measures. The tabulated correlations (italicised) are thus conservative estimates of the relationship between ability and attainment.

Very broadly, the results imply that a substantial element of national curriculum attainment (but albeit still only a part) may be predictable on the basis of factors beyond the immediate control of teachers. This should be taken into account when forming expectations about how well children should do on statutory tests. To facilitate this, further analysis of the data was conducted to equate, for each test, raw scores and national curriculum levels. These tables are presented on pages 50–3 of this manual.

Table 2: Correlations (Pearson's *r*) between national curriculum attainment and reasoning ability test results

National Curriculum assessment	Verbal Reasoning	Nonverbal Reasoning
English level	0.75	0.56
Reading level	0.73	0.65
Reading standardised score	*0.60*	*0.31*
Writing level	0.65	0.59
Spelling level	0.61	0.56
Spelling standardised score	*0.32*	*0.20*
Mathematics level	0.51	0.54
Mathematics standardised score	no data supplied	0.57
Written mathematics level	0.73	0.69
Written mathematics standardised score	*0.55*	*0.51*
Mental mathematics level	0.57	0.54
Mental mathematics standardised score	*0.47*	*0.48*
Science level	0.67	0.46

Reading Progress Tests

Denis Vincent, Mary Crumpler and Mike de la Mare

This innovative series of reading tests meets the need for continuous monitoring of reading progress throughout the primary school. The Reading Progress Tests provide a standardised *Literacy Baseline* and six reading comprehension tests, for Years 1 to 6. The tests can be used independently, but are most informative when used annually to provide an ongoing measure of attainment which can be related to the progress each child might be expected to make, year on year. They are thus particularly useful for identifying groups or individual children who, regardless of their actual level of reading ability, are making slower - or better - progress than is normal.

The **Reading Progress Tests** are quick to administer, taking just 45–50 minutes per class. The materials are attractively presented, using text and illustration to make the tests motivating and accessible to children across a wide ability range. *Standardised scores* and *reading ages* are provided for each year group.

STAGE ONE is for ages 5 to 8. The *Literacy Baseline* test, for use early in Year 1, is suitable for small-group or individual administration and covers important pre-reading and initial skills, including phonological awareness, print concepts, letter knowledge and simple decoding. It is designed for conventional screening, to identify children who lack the skills which underpin success in early literacy. *RPT1* and *RPT2*, for use towards the end of Year 1 and in Year 2, are group tests which assess developing reading skills and comprehension.

STAGE TWO provides a coherent series of reading comprehension tests for use in Years 3 to 6. *RPT3–6* are group tests which assess a wide range of literal and inferential skills and reading vocabulary, using test items and text passages of varying content and length. The reading passages are presented via full-colour broadsheets which can be reused with separate classes and/or from one year to the next.

Numeracy Progress Tests

Denis Vincent and Mary Crumpler

The **Numeracy Progress Tests** mirror the highly popular **Reading Progress Tests** in providing a baseline assessment plus year-on-year progress tests for use throughout the primary school. The tests can be used separately with selected year groups, but are most informative when used annually to provide an ongoing measure of attainment and progression: they are especially useful for identifying groups or individual children who are making slower – or better – progress than might be expected. The tests are quick and easy to use, taking just 45–50 minutes per class. The presentation is attractive and motivating to pupils, placing minimal reliance upon reading ability.

STAGE ONE is for ages 5 to 8. The *Numeracy Baseline* test, for use early in Year 1, assesses early numeracy skills and concepts, and consists of a group test supplemented by an optional, individually administered oral test. Where teachers are concerned about particular children, this may be used to assess their readiness for taking the main group test. It also covers skills not amenable to group written testing, and may be used where a comprehensive assessment is required. *NPT1* and *NPT2* are group tests designed for use towards the end of Years 1 and 2, respectively.

STAGE TWO, for ages 7 to 12, provides a coherent series of group tests suitable for end-of-year monitoring in each of Years 3 to 6, with a carefully controlled progression in content which is consistent with the numeracy elements of the national curriculum for mathematics.

Norms are given as *standardised scores* and *numeracy age* equivalents based on the performance of 8000 children drawn from a national sample of schools in England and Wales, and as *national curriculum levels.*

RSPT Reasoning Progress Test

V 3

Name: .... *Boy/Girl*

School: ....

Class: .... *Date of birth:* .... *Date of test:* ....

AGE: YEARS.........	COMPLETED MONTHS.........	RAW SCORE TOTAL.........	STANDARDISED SCORE.........

New words for old

Make two new words. Make the first one by taking one letter from the first bold word. Make the second by adding that letter to the second bold word. Don't change the order of the letters. Draw a line under the two new words - one from each group of words in brackets.

Practice

SCREAM and **TABLE** make
(SCRAM CRAMS CREAM CREASE)
and (STABLE SABLE TABLET CABLE).

RSPT Reasoning Progress Test

NV 3

Name: .... *Boy/Girl*

School: ....

Class: .... *Date of birth:* .... *Date of test:* ....

AGE: YEARS.........	COMPLETED MONTHS.........	RAW SCORE TOTAL.........	STANDARDISED SCORE.........

Find the fourth shape

Which shape in the right-hand box is most similar to the three shapes in the left-hand box? Draw a line under your answer.

Practice

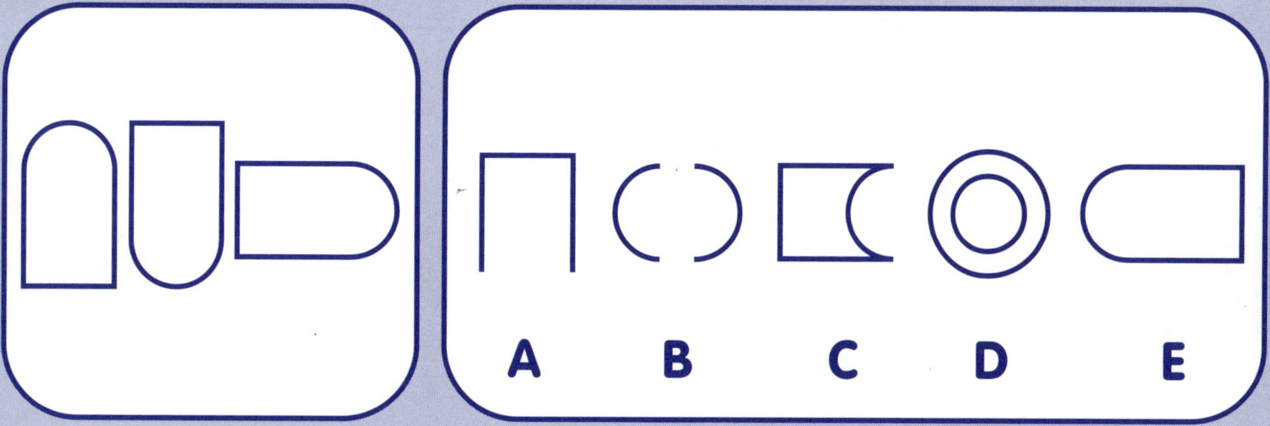

1

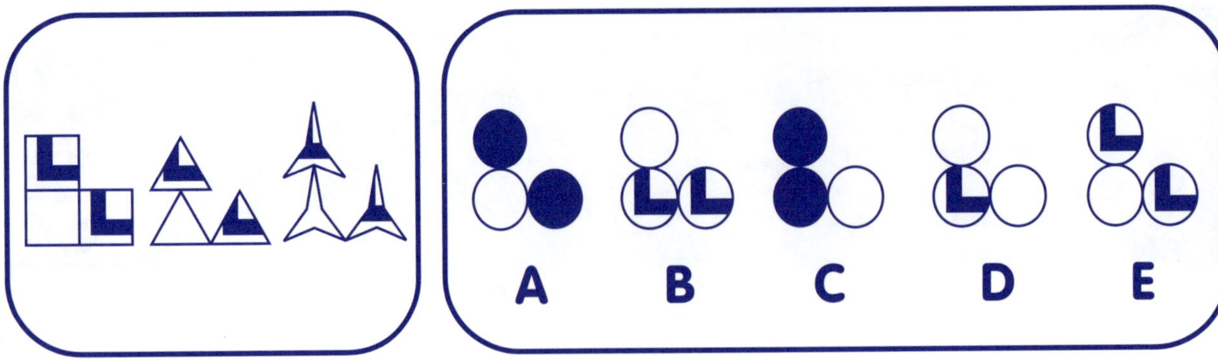

2

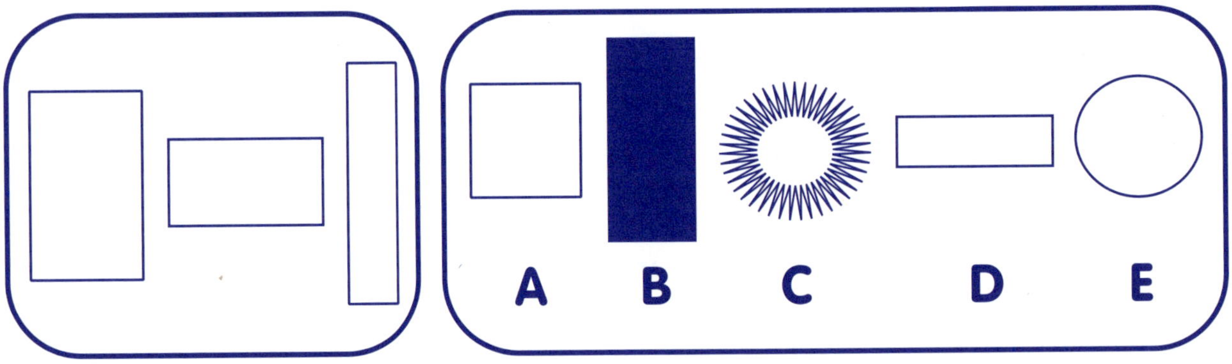

3

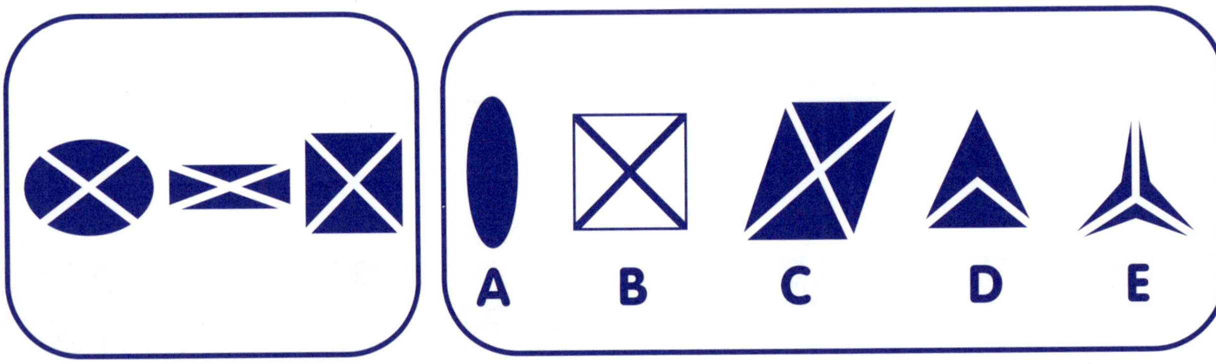

4

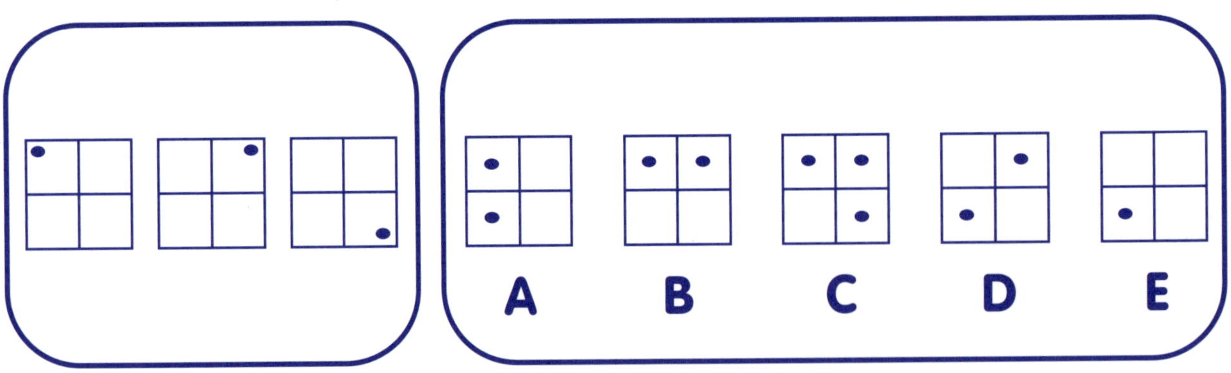

5

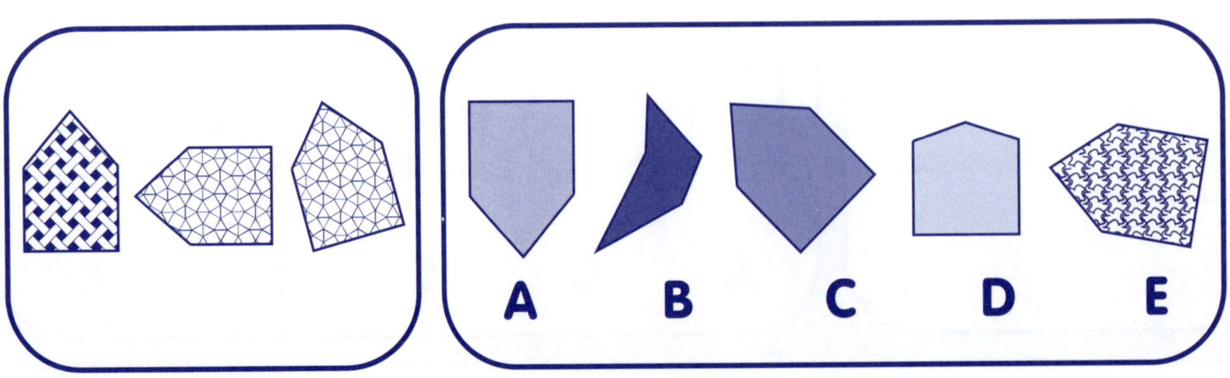

Reasoning Progress Test

NV 3

Name: .... Boy/Girl

School: ....

Class: .... Date of birth: .... Date of test: ....

AGE:	COMPLETED	RAW SCORE	STANDARDISED
YEARS.........	MONTHS.........	TOTAL.........	SCORE.........

Find the fourth shape

Which shape in the right-hand box is most similar to the three shapes in the left-hand box? Draw a line under your answer.

Practice

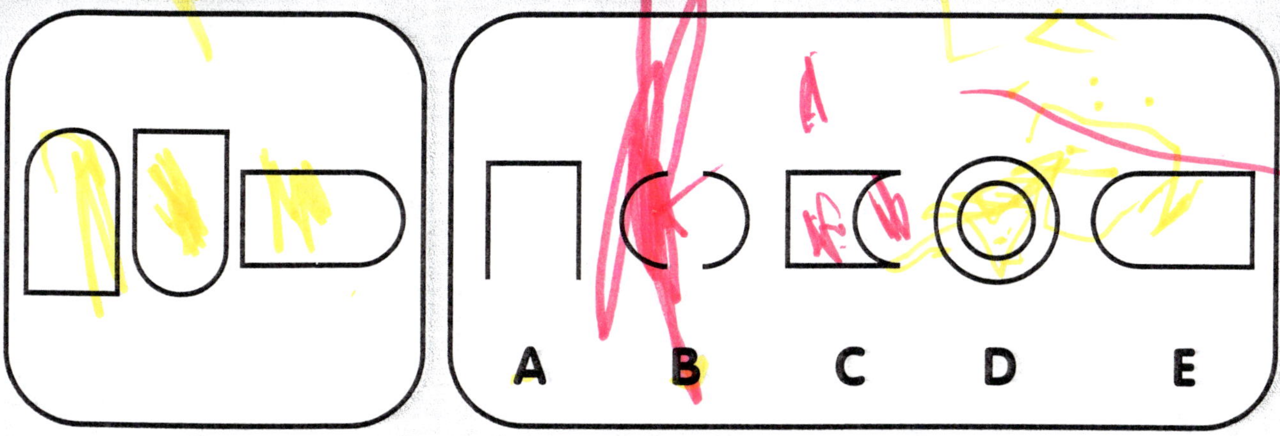

1

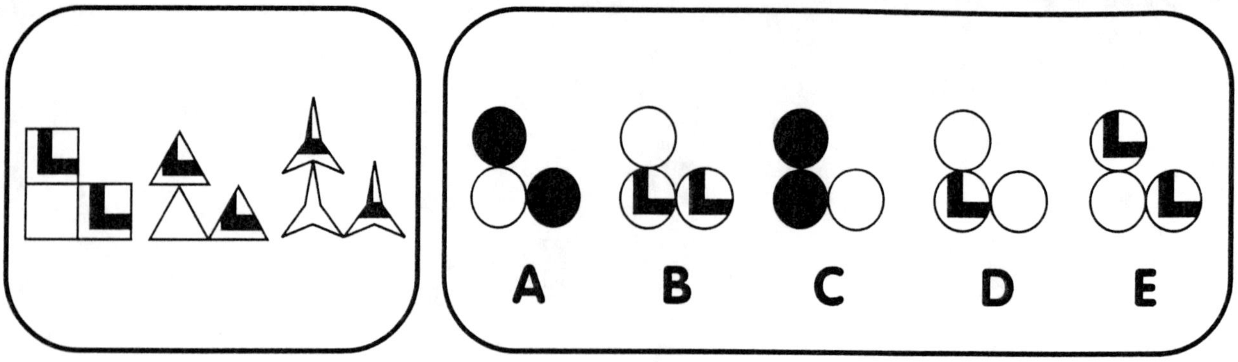

2

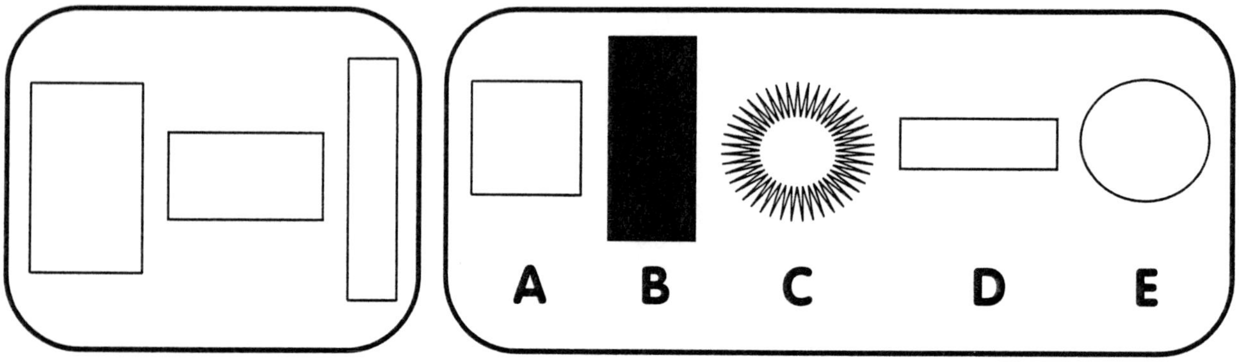

3

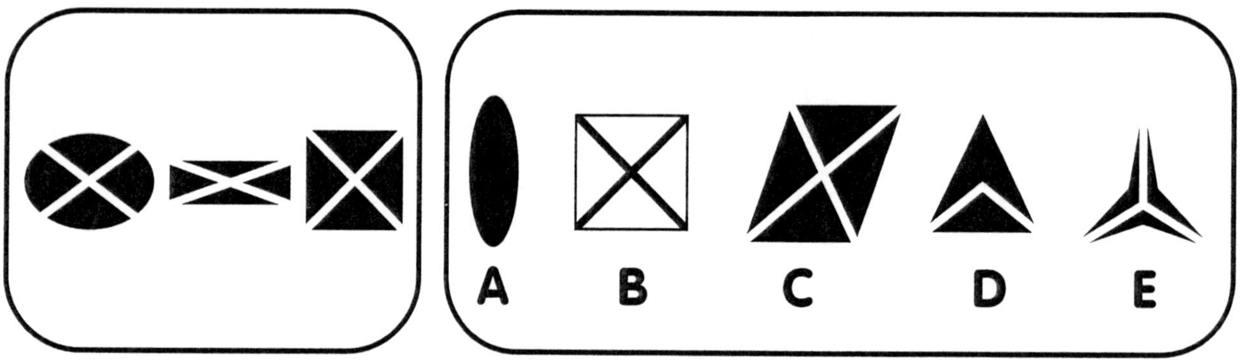

4

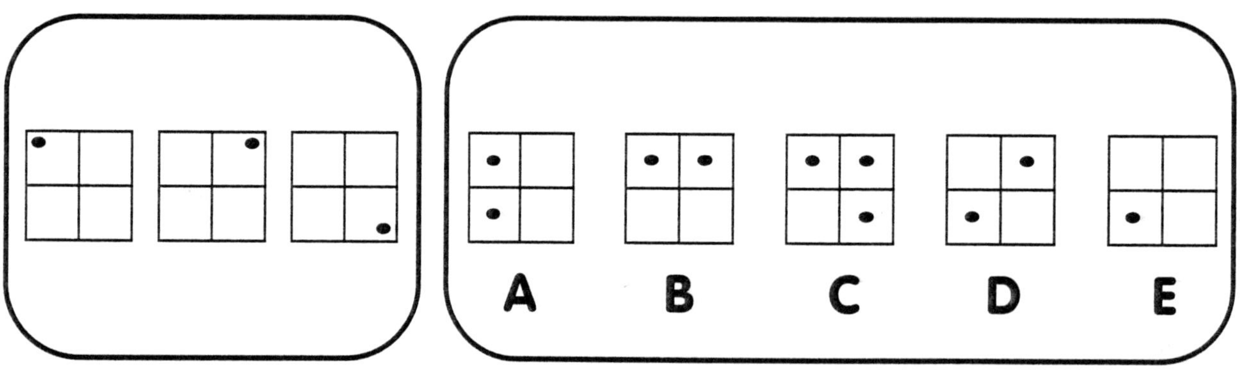

5

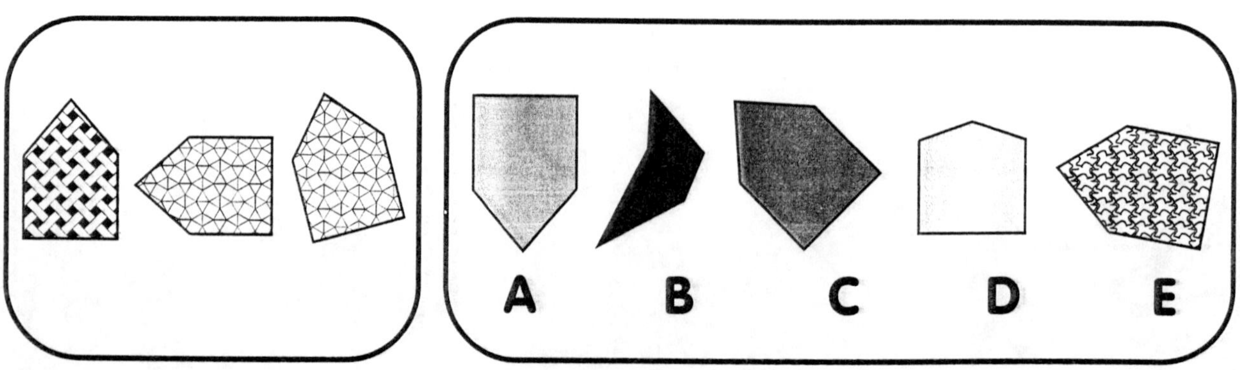

Folding

Look at the shape in the first box. Imagine that it has been folded along the dotted line. Which of the five shapes on the right would it look like when it has been folded? Draw a line under your answer.

Practice

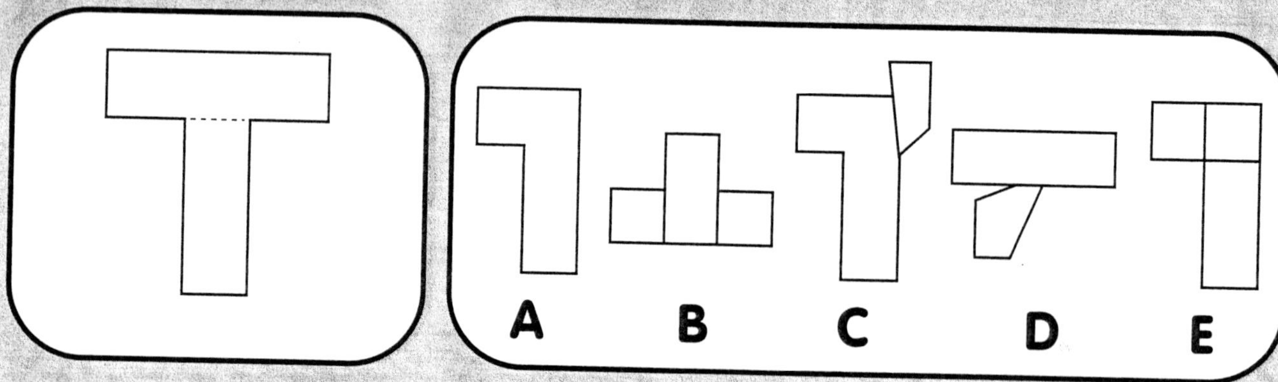

11

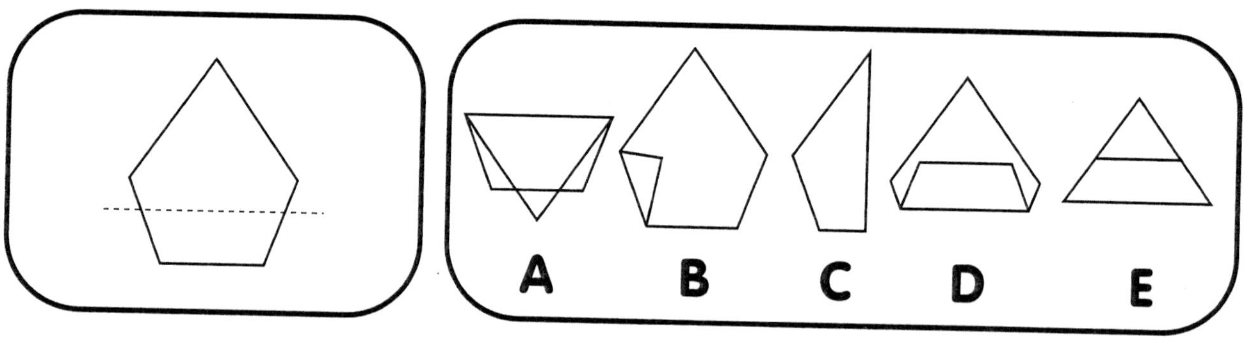

12

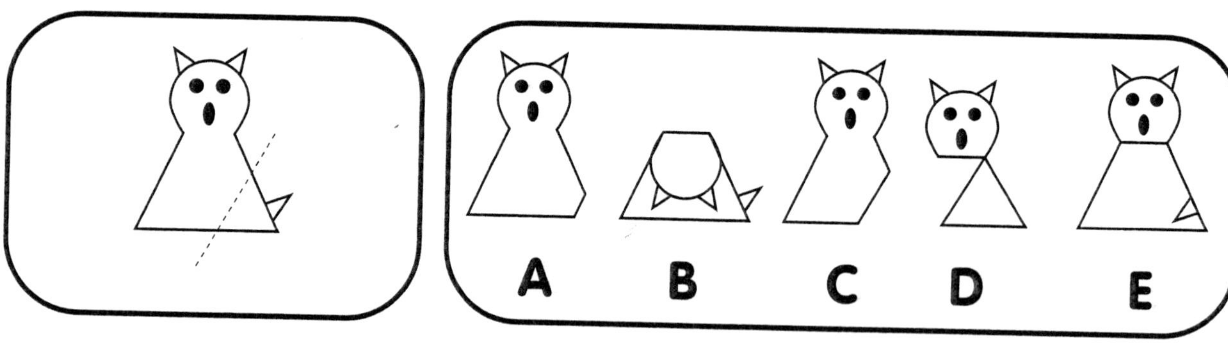

13

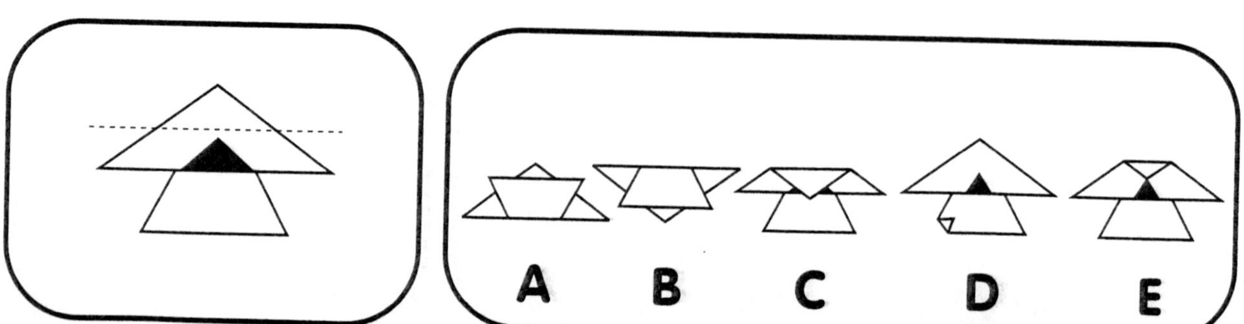

Odd one out

Which is the odd one out? Draw a line under your answer.

Practice

20

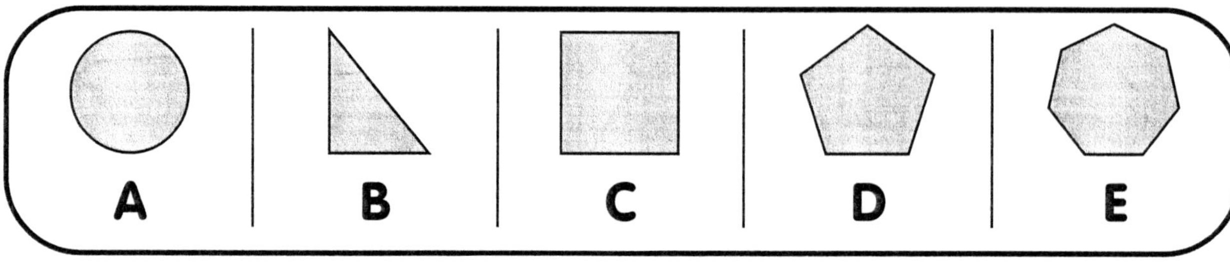

21

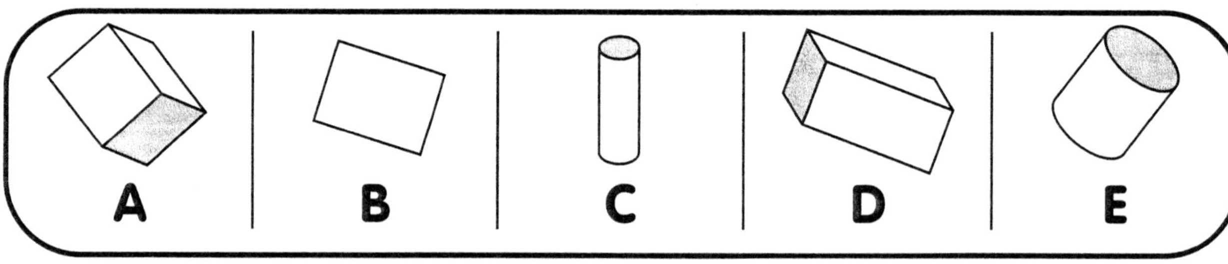

22

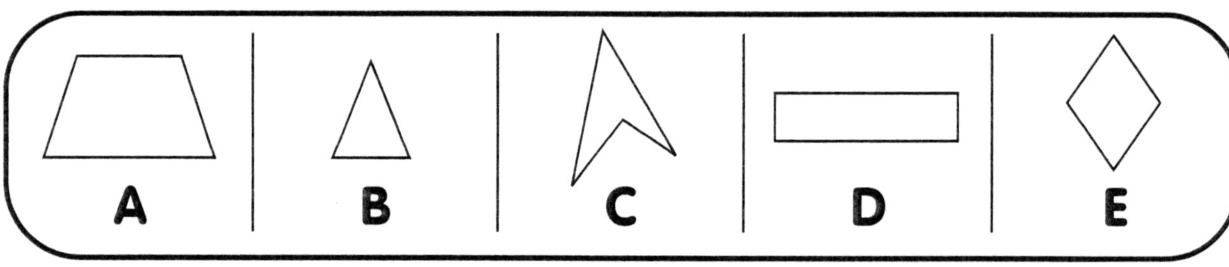

23

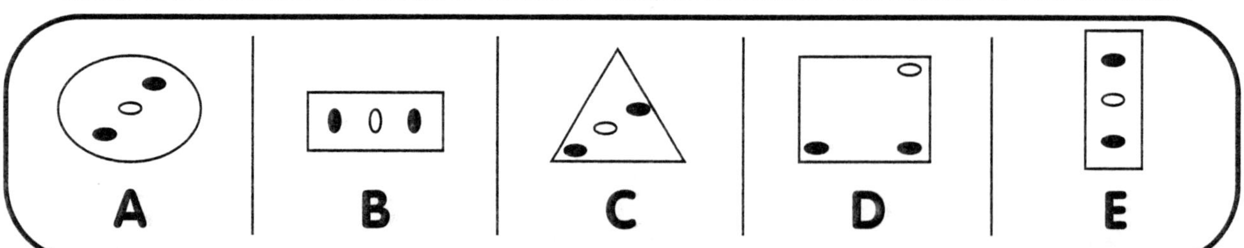

24

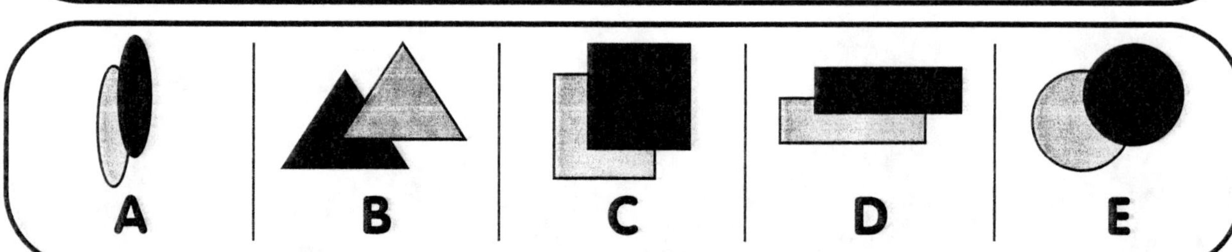

What's missing?

Which shape in the right-hand box correctly completes the picture in the left-hand box? Draw a line under your answer.

Practice

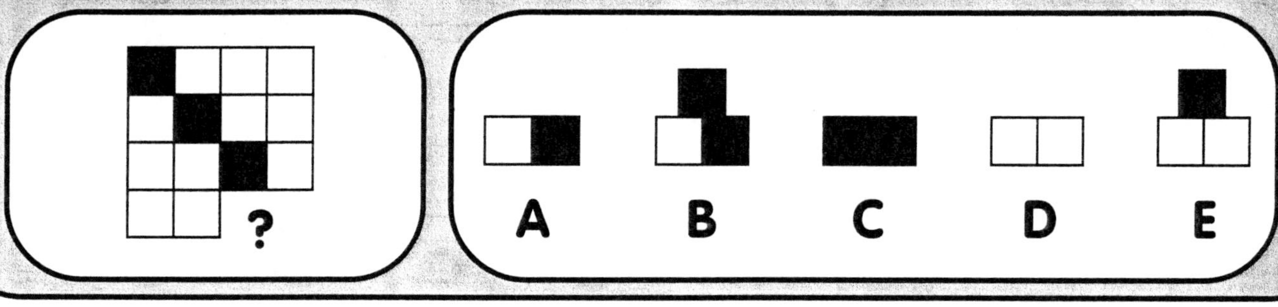

25

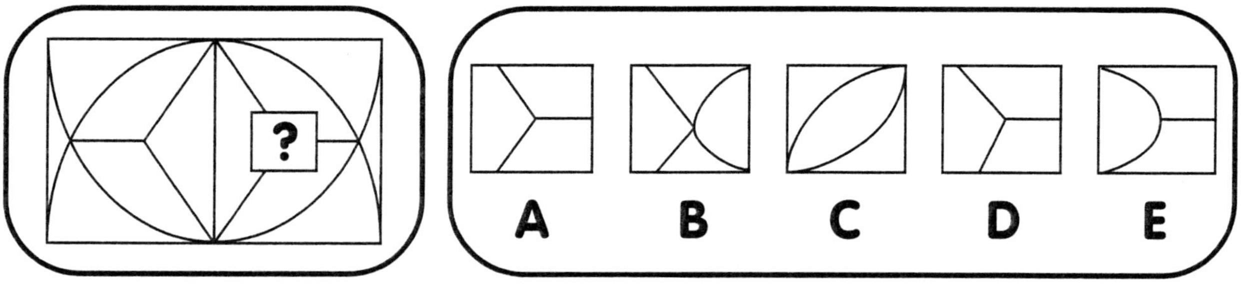

26

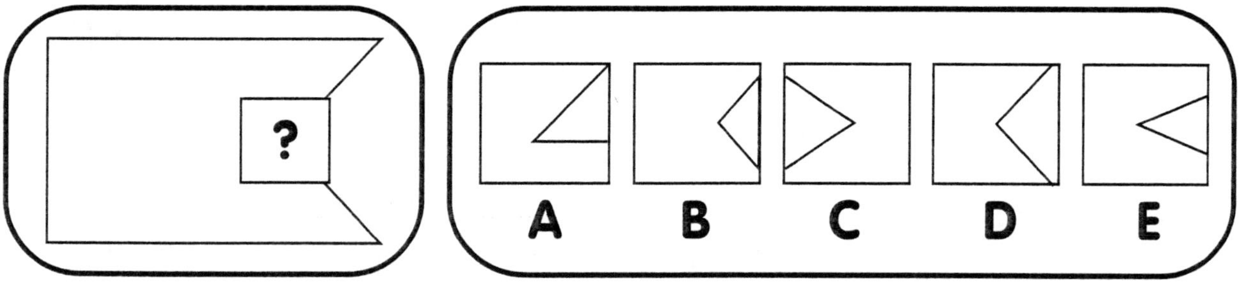

27

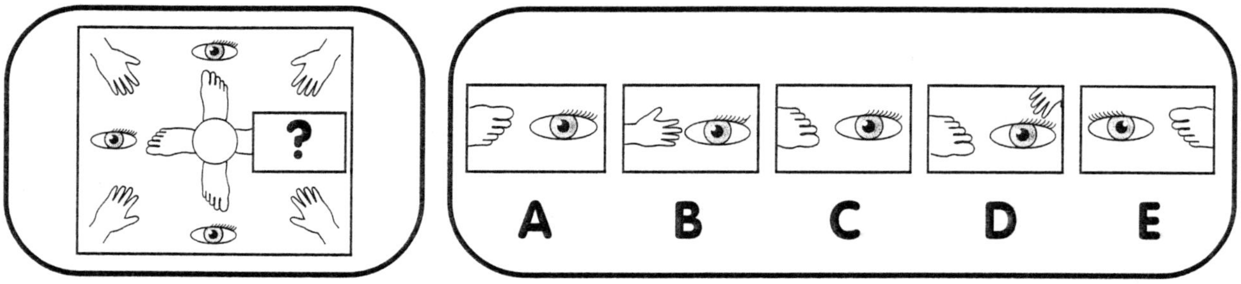

28

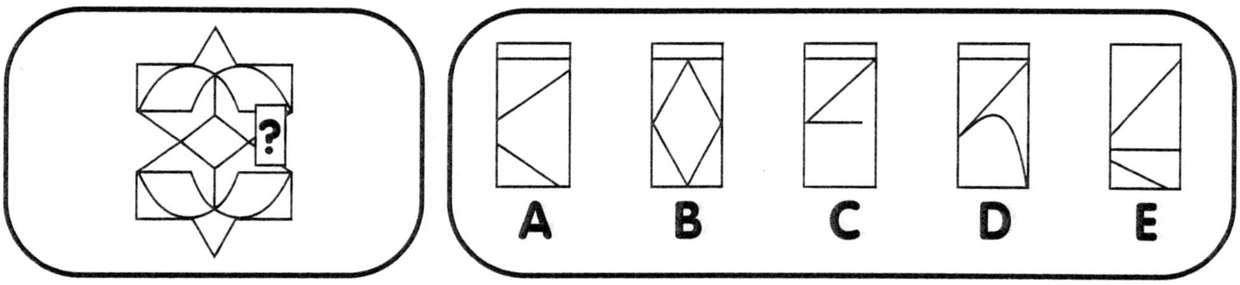

14

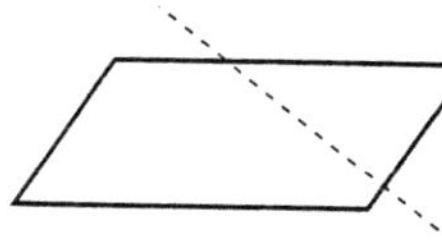

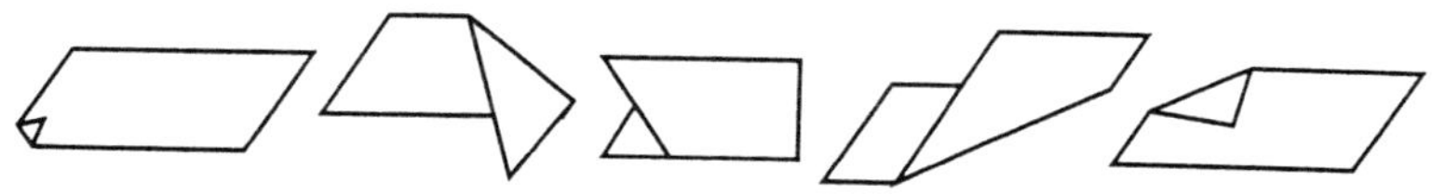

A B C D E

15

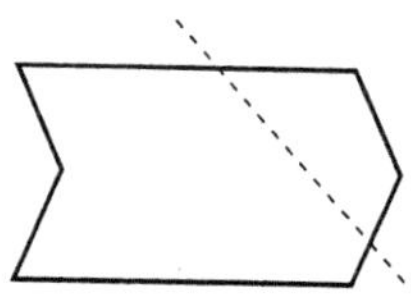

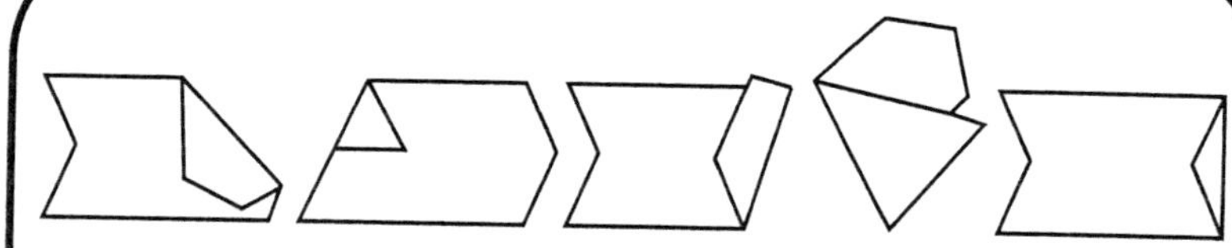

A B C D E

16

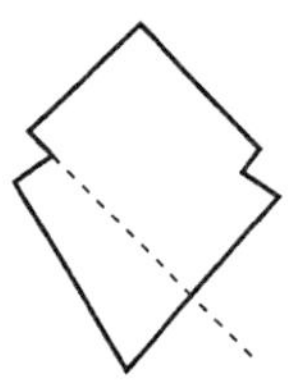

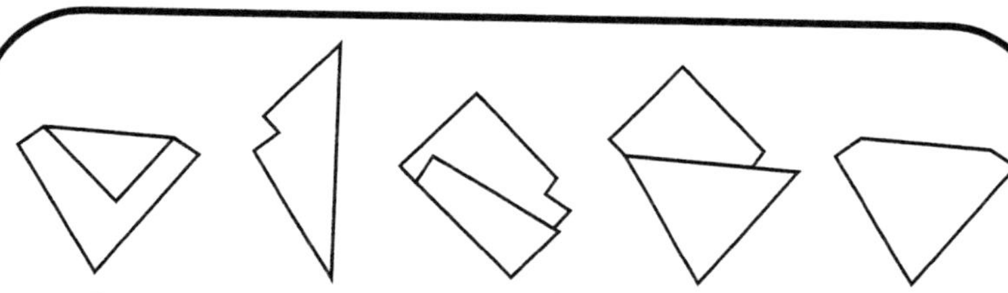

A B C D E

17

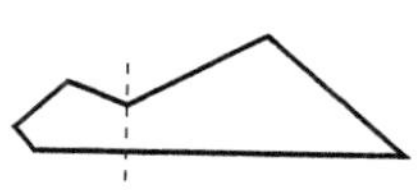

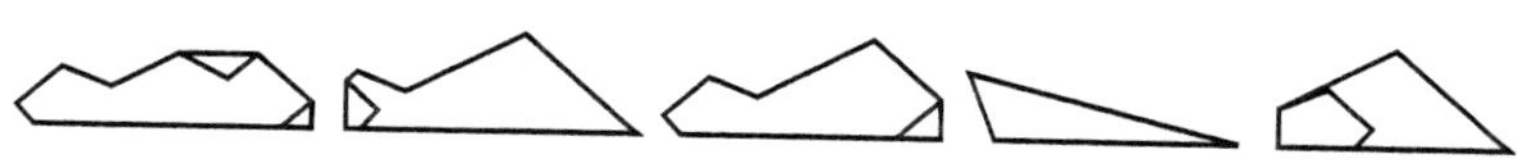

A B C D E

18

A B C D E

19

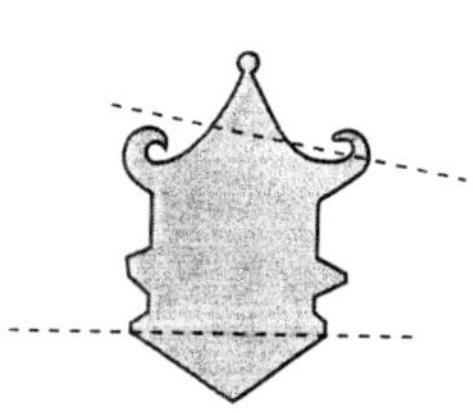

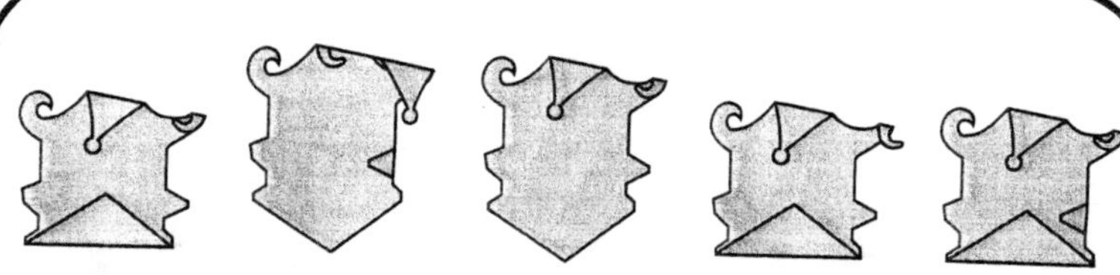

A B C D E

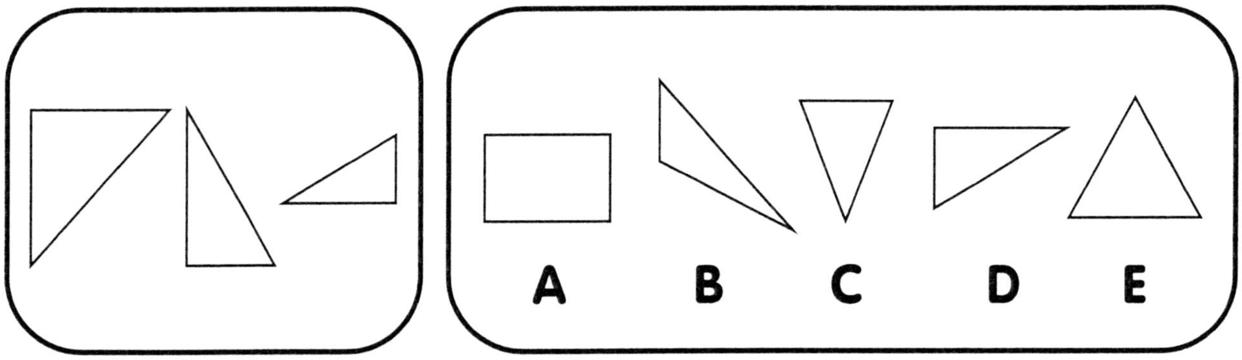
A
B
C
D
E

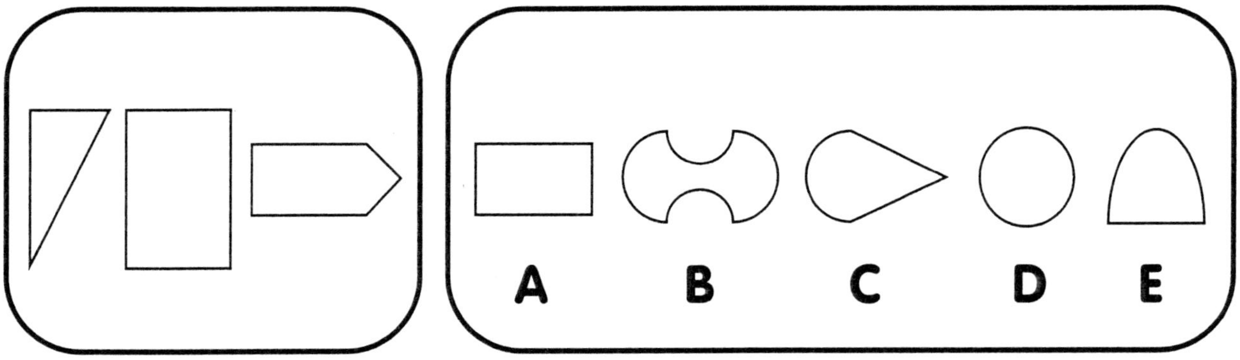
A
B
C
D
E

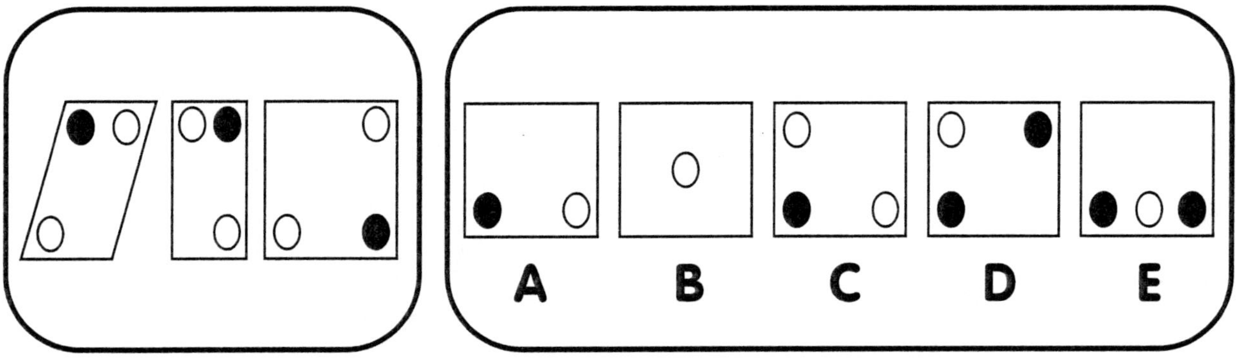
A
B
C
D
E

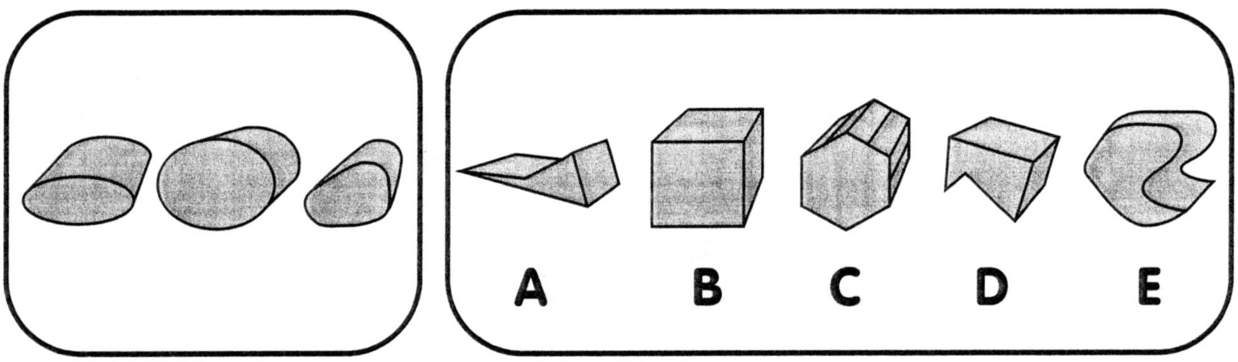
A
B
C
D
E

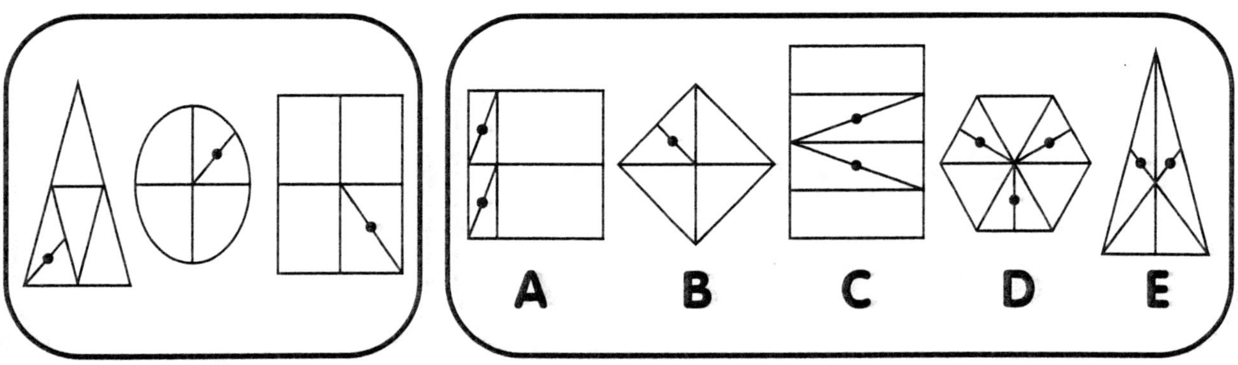
A
B
C
D
E

29 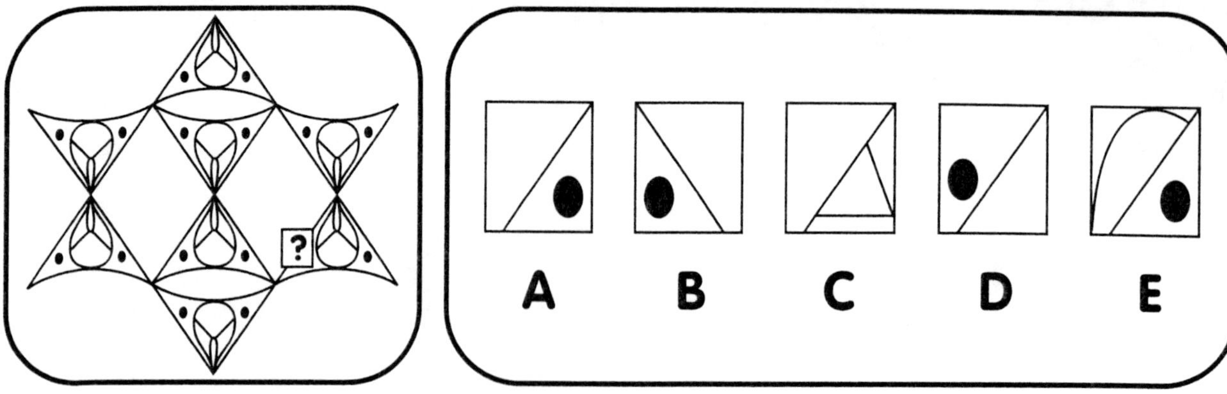

30 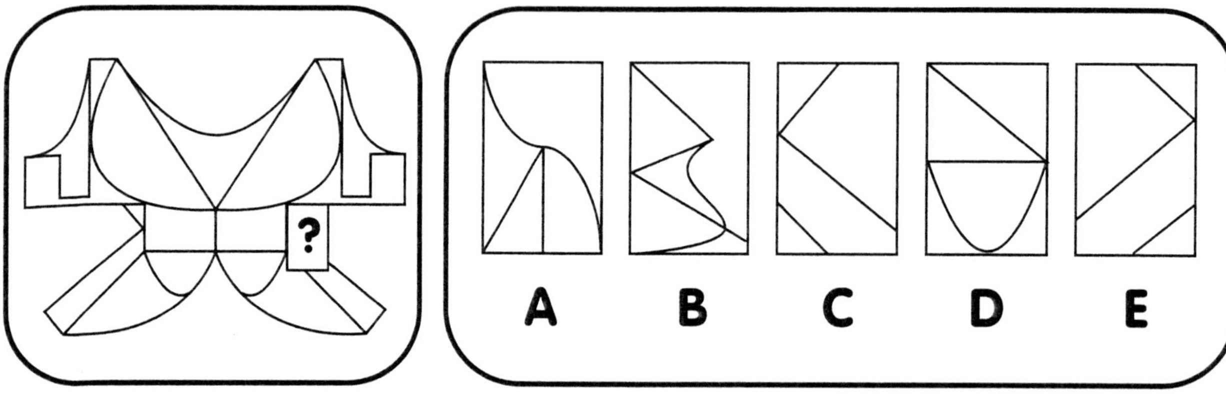

31 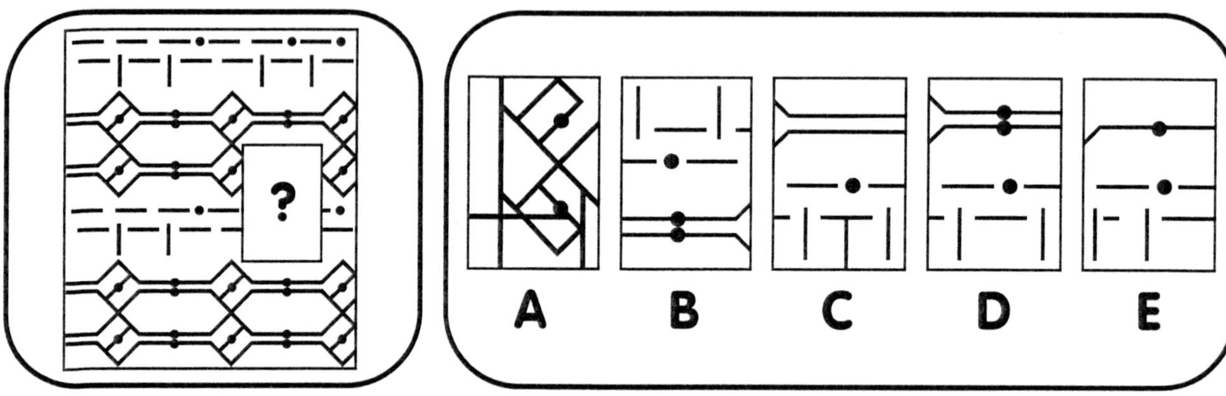

32 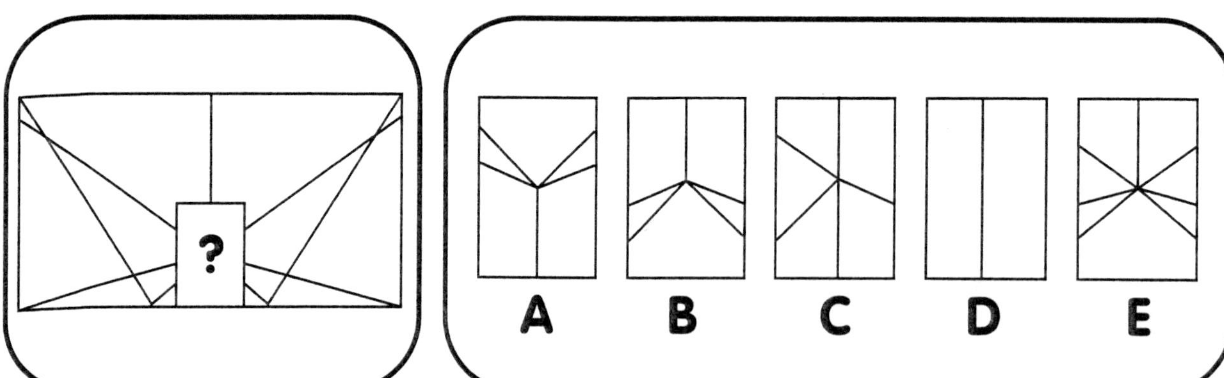

ISBN 0 340 85885 0 (*pack of 10 copies*)

Impression number 10 9 8 7 6 5 4 3 2 1
Year 2007 2006 2005 2004 2003 2002

Printed in Great Britain for Hodder & Stoughton Educational, a division of Hodder Headline Plc, 338 Euston Road, London NW1 3BH, by Hobbs the Printers Ltd, Brunel Road, Totton, Hampshire SO40 3WX.

6

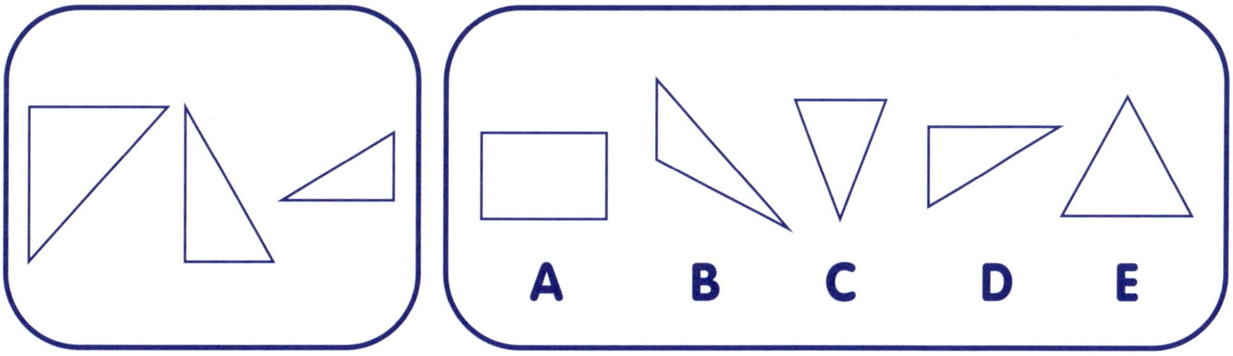

7

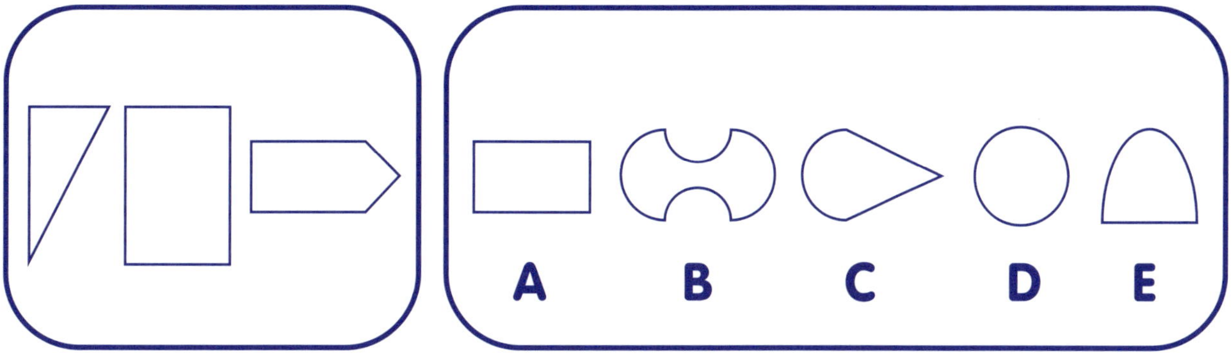

8

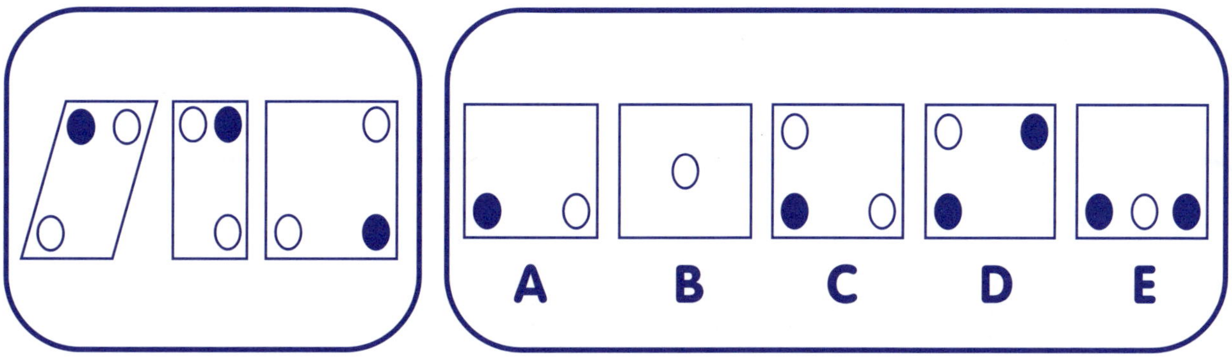

9

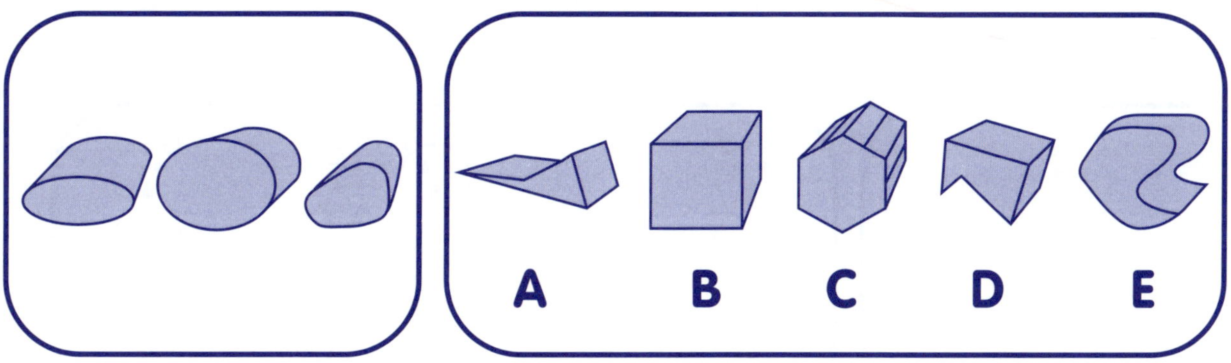

0

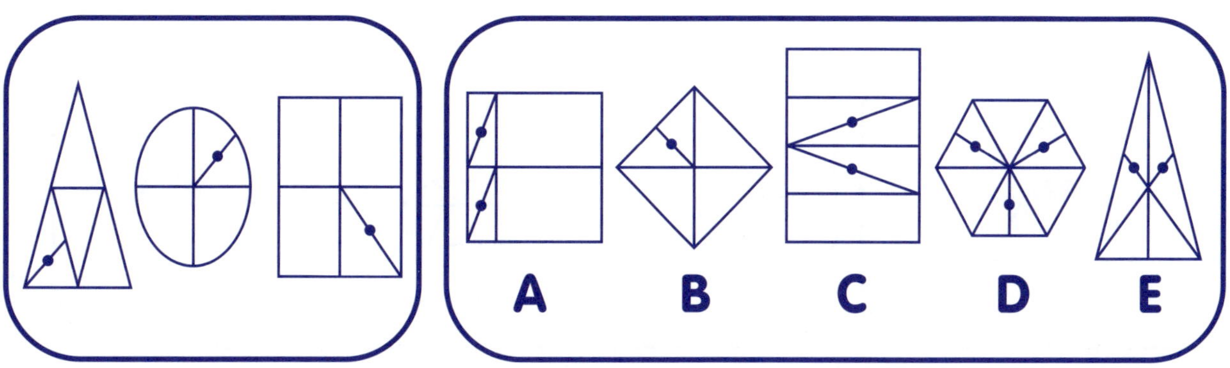

Folding

Look at the shape in the first box. Imagine that it has been folded along the dotted line. Which of the five shapes on the right would it look like when it has been folded? Draw a line under your answer.

Practice

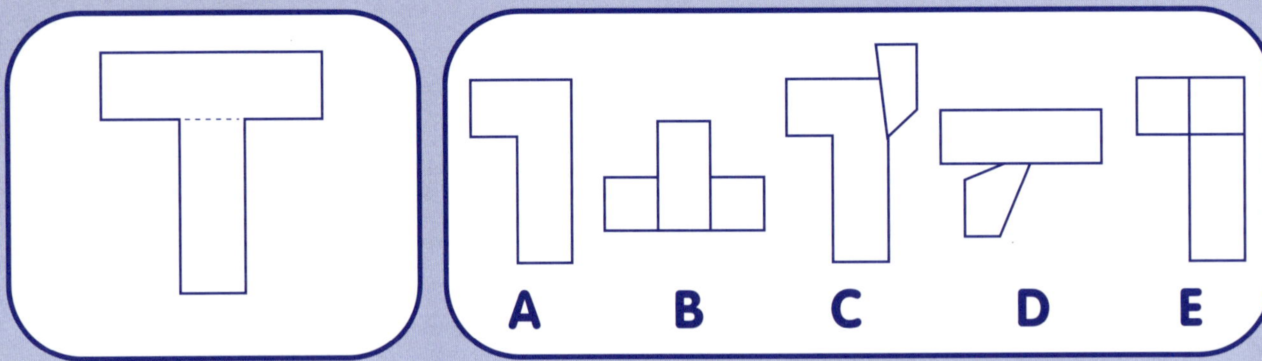

11
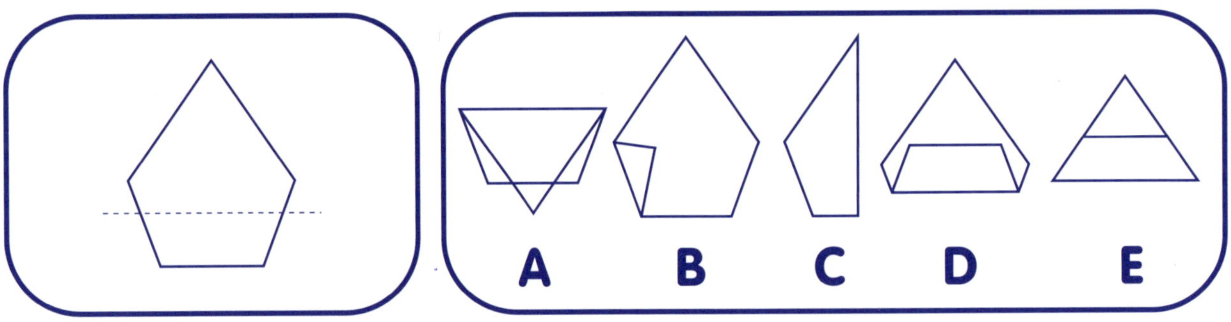

12
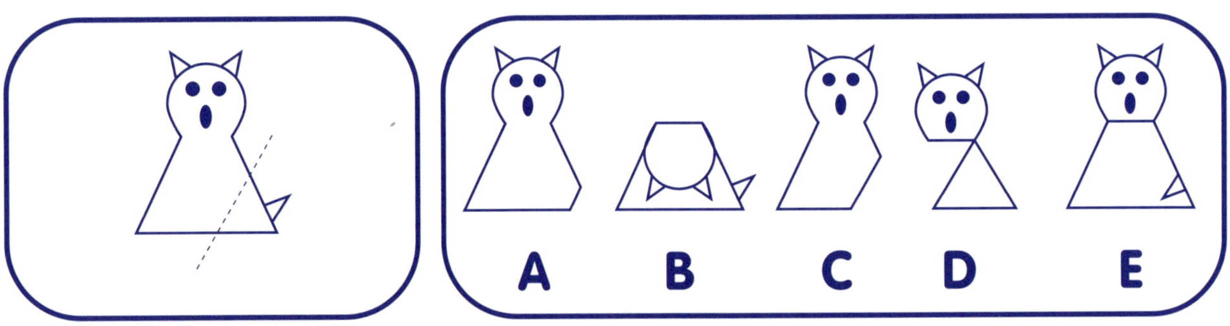

13
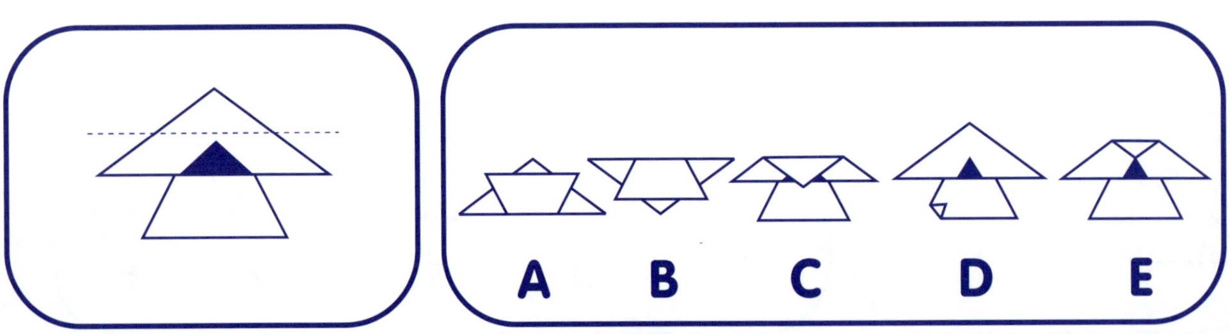

14
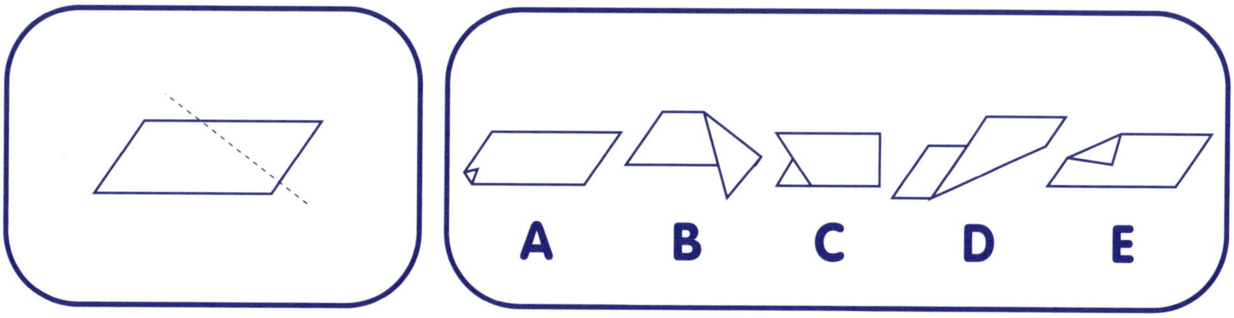

15
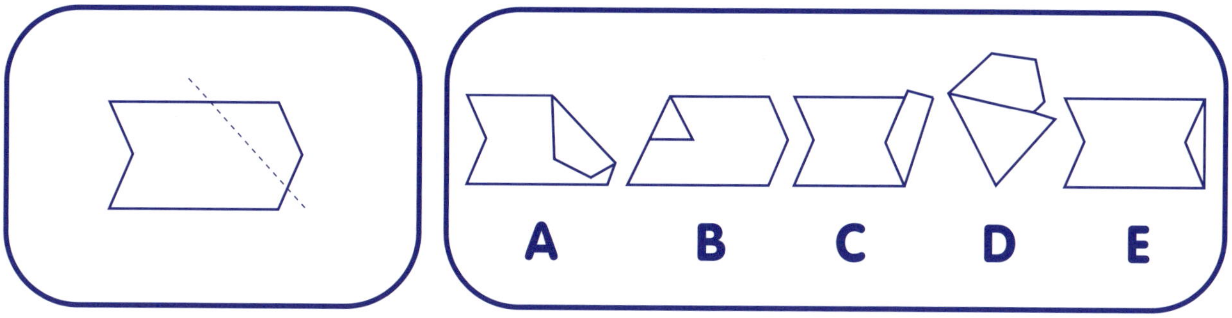

16
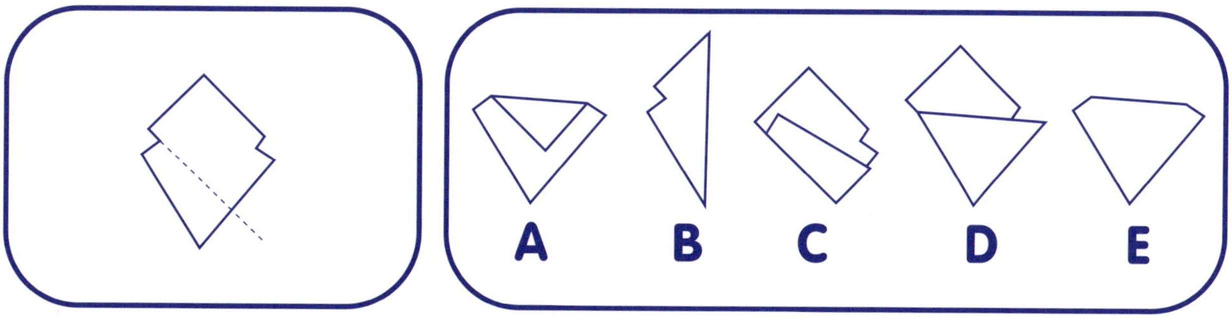

17
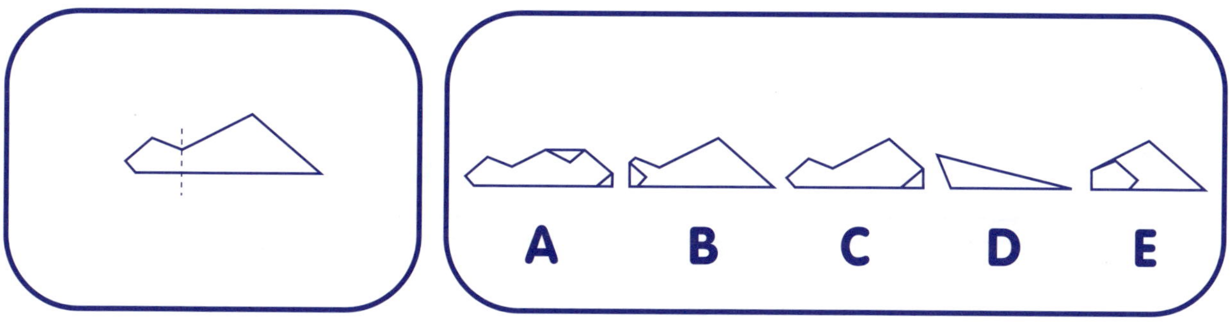

18
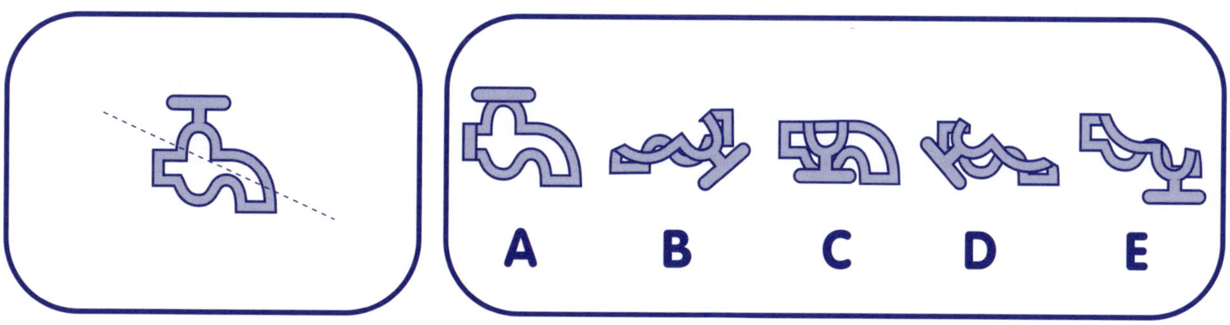

19
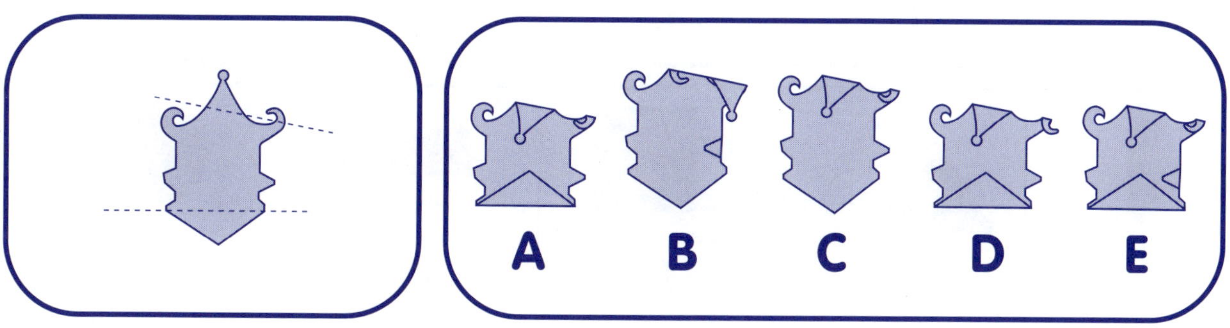

Odd one out

Which is the odd one out? Draw a line under your answer.

Practice

20

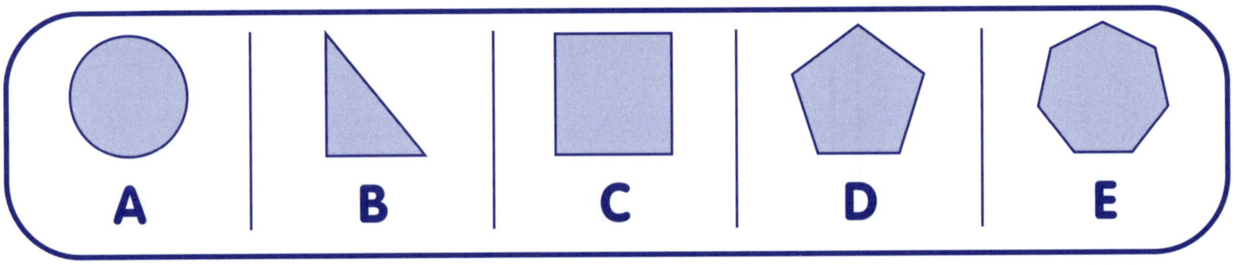

21

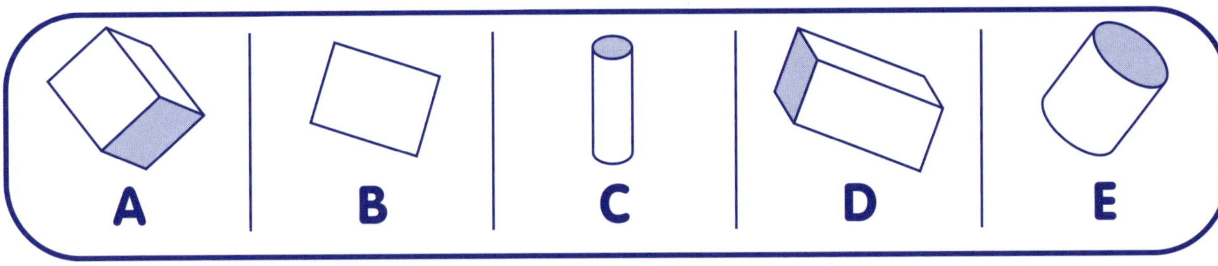

22

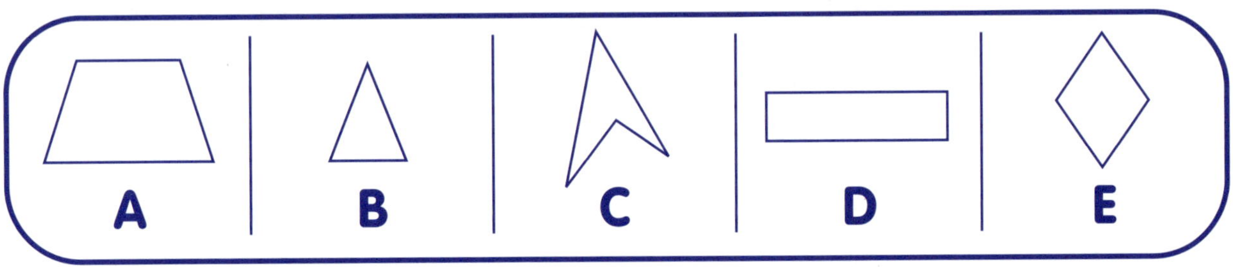

23

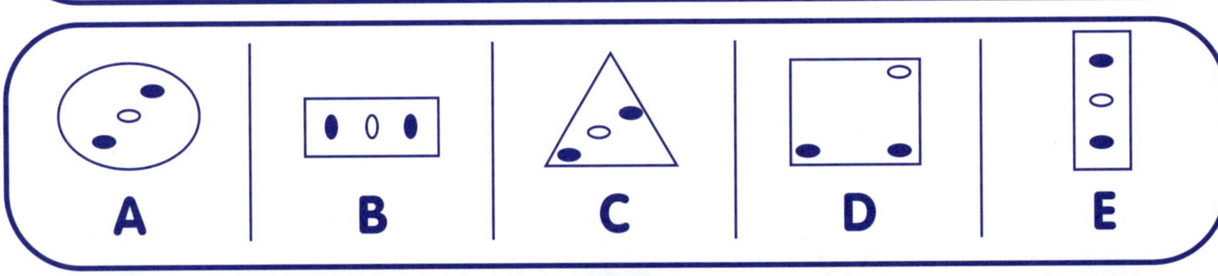

24

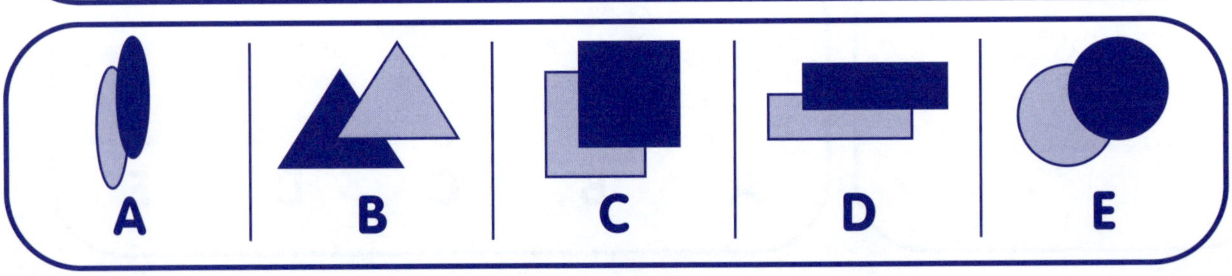

What's missing?

Which shape in the right-hand box correctly completes the picture in the left-hand box? Draw a line under your answer.

Practice

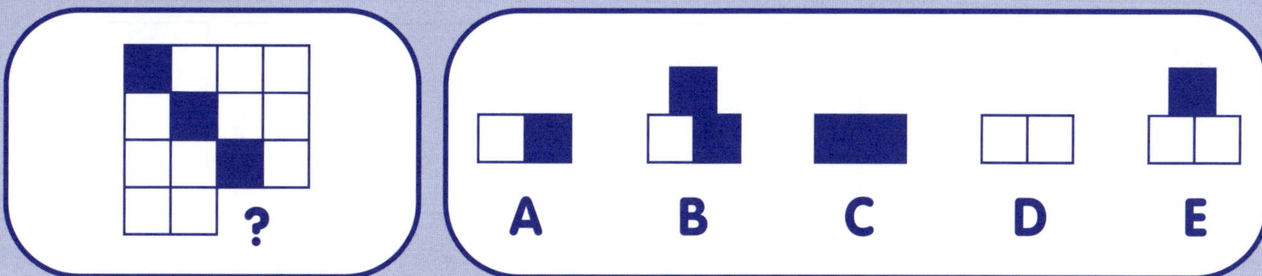

25

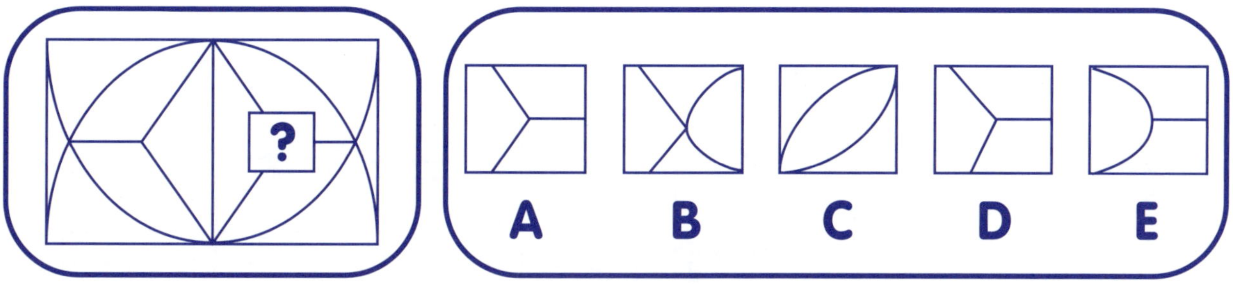

26

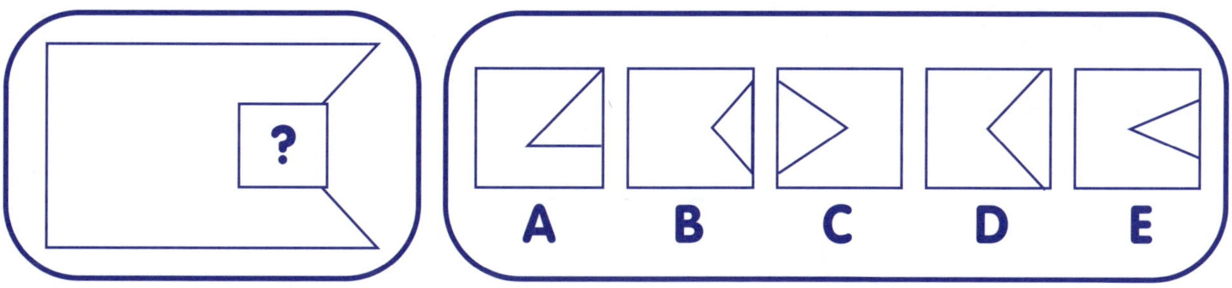

27

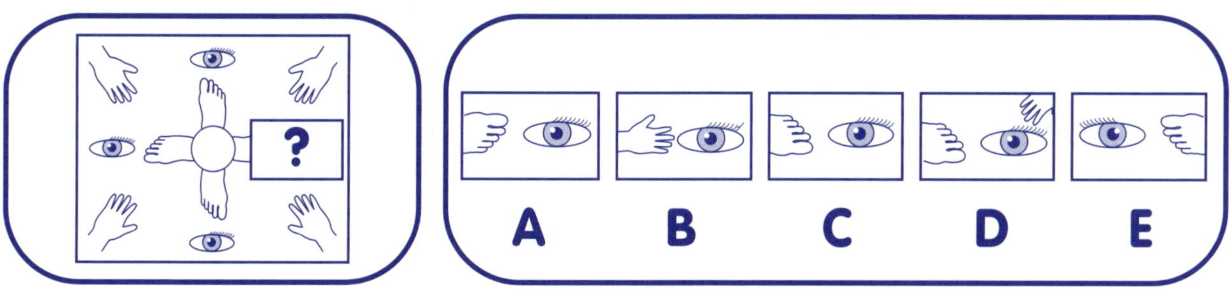

28

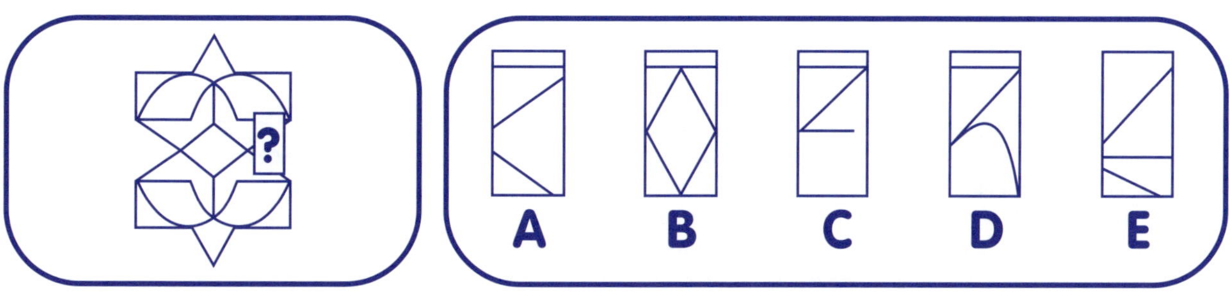

29

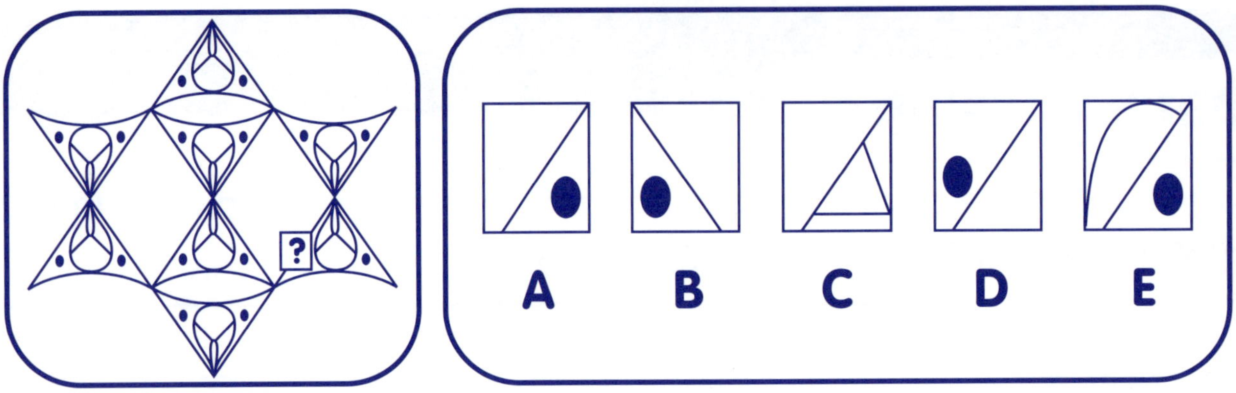

30

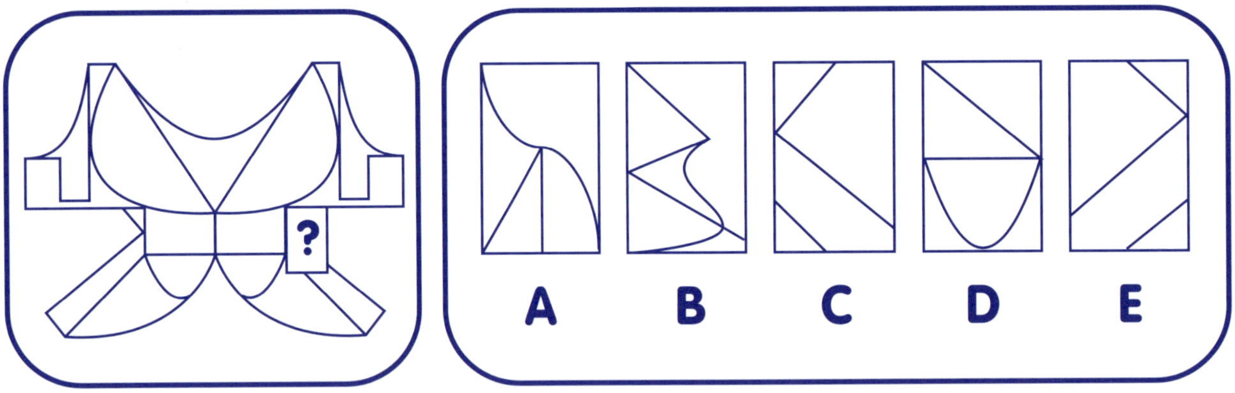

31

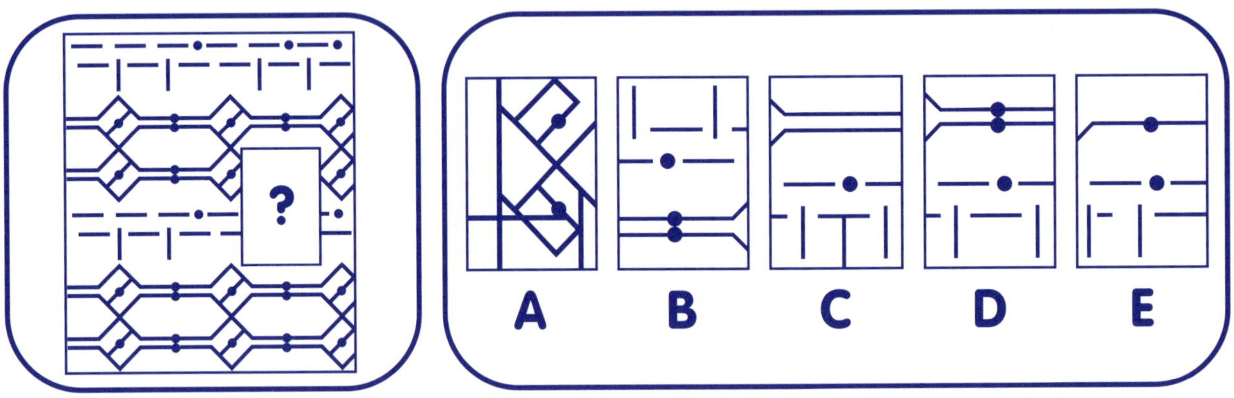

32

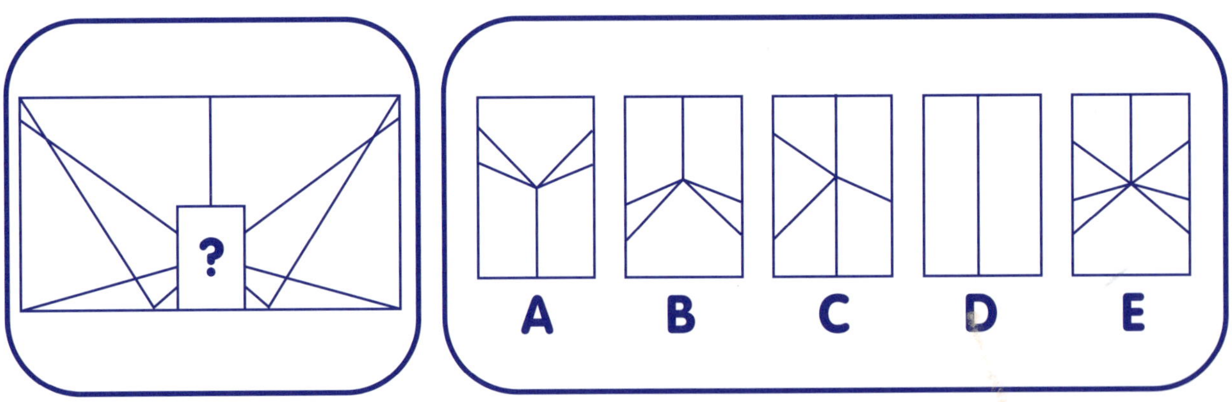

ISBN 0 340 85885 0 (*pack of 10 copies*)

Impression number 10 9 8 7 6 5 4 3 2 1
Year 2007 2006 2005 2004 2003 2002

Printed in Great Britain for Hodder & Stoughton Educational, a division of Hodder Headline Plc, 338 Euston Road, London NW1 3BH, by Hobbs the Printers Ltd, Brunel Road, Totton, Hampshire SO40 3WX.

Which picture?

Which picture matches the word? Draw a line under your answer

Practice

domestic

A B C D

21 appropriate

A B C D

22 expressionless

A B C D

23 amused

A B C D

24 hollow

A B C D

Complete the sentence

Which word in the brackets completes the sentence?
Draw a line under the word you have chosen.

Practice

Clock is to hours
as calendar is to (pictures months birthdays organise).

8 Toes are to feet
as (fingers catching gloves arms) are to hands.

9 Scissors are to cut
as (drawing pencil paper book) is to write.

10 Rough is to sandpaper
as (dress smooth material cotton) is to silk.

11 Trunk is to tree
as stem is to (bush plant root bud).

12 Spiders are to eight
as tigers are to (fierce four furry animals).

13 Hamsters are to home
as sheep are to (zoo farm field garden).

New words for old

Make two new words. Make the first one by taking one letter from the first bold word. Make the second by adding that letter to the second bold word. Don't change the order of the letters. Draw a line under the two new words - one from each group of words in brackets.

Practice

SCREAM and **TABLE** make
(SCRAM CRAMS CREAM CREASE)
and (STABLE SABLE TABLET CABLE).

SLIT and **TONE** make
(LIST STILL LIT SIT)
and (TON STRONG NOT STONE).

PRIDE and **RAISE** make
(RICE DIRE RIDE DEER)
and (PRIZE DAISY PRAISE PRICE).

BEAT and **RAKE** make
(TEA EAT ATE BEE)
and (TEAR BAKE BRAKE TAKE).

SLIGHT and **PAN** make
(LIGHT SIGHT HIGH PLIGHT)
and (PLAN PANG PANT PAIN).

LIMP and **CAP** make
(LIMB LAND LAP LIP)
and (LAMP CAMP CLAMP CRAMP).

THREE and **ANGER** make
(TREAT THERE TWO TREE)
and (HANGER RANGER ANGLER TRIANGLE).

CAREER and **BREATH** make
(RACER CARE CAR CARER)
and (BREAD BREATHE BREAKER BEACH).

More new words

A single letter changes in the first word to get to the second word.
One letter also changes in the second word to get to the third word.
Draw a line under the word which would be the second word.

Practice

break – ? – cream	brake	bread	creak	wreak

fair – ? – pain	pair	lair	fail	pail
come – ? – dame	camp	dome	damp	cone
boat – ? – seat	bolt	beat	salt	best
wail – ? – bait	wait	pail	beat	wall
hear – ? – team	heat	tear	hare	beam
malt – ? – maze	wine	male	salt	gaze
shark – ? – stare	share	shard	shirk	start

Find the general word

Which is the general word? Draw a line under your answer.

Practice

sense smell touch sight hearing taste

25 sound ring whistle scream music bang ____

26 knife utensil spoon whisk spatula ladle ____

27 day century second period minute fortnight ____

28 Surrey Sussex Antrim Lanarkshire County Pembrokeshire ____

29 glow light flash glimmer spark beam ____

SLIT and **TONE** make
(LIST STILL LIT SIT)
and (TON STRONG NOT STONE).

PRIDE and **RAISE** make
(RICE DIRE RIDE DEER)
and (PRIZE DAISY PRAISE PRICE).

BEAT and **RAKE** make
(TEA EAT ATE BEE)
and (TEAR BAKE BRAKE TAKE).

SLIGHT and **PAN** make
(LIGHT SIGHT HIGH PLIGHT)
and (PLAN PANG PANT PAIN).

LIMP and **CAP** make
(LIMB LAND LAP LIP)
and (LAMP CAMP CLAMP CRAMP).

THREE and **ANGER** make
(TREAT THERE TWO TREE)
and (HANGER RANGER ANGLER TRIANGLE).

CAREER and **BREATH** make
(RACER CARE CAR CARER)
and (BREAD BREATHE BREAKER BEACH).

Complete the sentence

Which word in the brackets completes the sentence?
Draw a line under the word you have chosen.

Practice

Clock is to hours
as calendar is to (pictures months birthdays organise).

8 Toes are to feet
as (fingers catching gloves arms) are to hands.

9 Scissors are to cut
as (drawing pencil paper book) is to write.

10 Rough is to sandpaper
as (dress smooth material cotton) is to silk.

11 Trunk is to tree
as stem is to (bush plant root bud).

12 Spiders are to eight
as tigers are to (fierce four furry animals).

13 Hamsters are to home
as sheep are to (zoo farm field garden).

More new words

A single letter changes in the first word to get to the second word.
One letter also changes in the second word to get to the third word.
Draw a line under the word which would be the second word.

Practice

break – ? – cream	brake	bread	creak	wreak

fair – ? – pain	pair	lair	fail	pail
come – ? – dame	camp	dome	damp	cone
boat – ? – seat	bolt	beat	salt	best
wail – ? – bait	wait	pail	beat	wall
hear – ? – team	heat	tear	hare	beam
malt – ? – maze	wine	male	salt	gaze
shark – ? – stare	share	shard	shirk	start

Which picture?

Which picture matches the word? Draw a line under your answer

Practice

domestic

A B C D

21 appropriate

A B C D

22 expressionless

A B C D

23 amused

A B C D

24 hollow

A B C D

Find the general word

Which is the general word? Draw a line under your answer.

Practice

sense smell touch sight hearing taste

5 sound ring whistle scream music bang

6 knife utensil spoon whisk spatula ladle

7 day century second period minute fortnight

8 Surrey Sussex Antrim Lanarkshire County Pembrokeshire

9 glow light flash glimmer spark beam

ISBN 0 340 85886 9 (*pack of 10 copies*)

Impression number 10 9 8 7 6 5 4 3 2 1
Year 2007 2006 2005 2004 2003 2002

Printed in Great Britain for Hodder & Stoughton Educational, a division of Hodder Headline Plc, 338 Euston Road, London NW1 3BH, by Hobbs the Printers Ltd, Brunel Road, Totton, Hampshire SO40 3WX.